The
Anti-Monopoly
Persuasion

The
Anti-Monopoly
Persuasion _____

POPULAR RESISTANCE
TO THE RISE OF
BIG BUSINESS
IN THE MIDWEST _____

Steven L. Piott

**CONTRIBUTIONS IN ECONOMICS AND
ECONOMIC HISTORY, NUMBER** 60
Greenwood Press
WESTPORT, CONNECTICUT · LONDON, ENGLAND

Library of Congress Cataloging in Publication Data

Piott, Steven L.
   The anti-monopoly persuasion.

   (Contributions in economics and economic history,
ISSN 0084-9235 ; no. 60)
   Bibliography: p.
   Includes index.
   1. Monopolies—Middle West—History.   2. Trusts,
Industrial—Middle West—History.   3. Big business—
Middle West—Public opinion—History.   4. Public opinion—
Middle West—History.   I. Title.   II. Series.
HD2798.A14P56   1985   338.8'2'0977   84-15694
ISBN 0-313-24545-2 (lib. bdg.)

Library of Congress Catalog Card Number: 84-15694
ISBN: 0-313-24545-2
ISSN: 0084-9235

First published in 1985

Greenwood Press
A division of Congressional Information Service, Inc.
88 Post Road West
Westport, Connecticut 06881

Printed in the United States of America

10 9 8 7 6 5 4 3 2 1

To Susan Eckhardt

CONTENTS

ACKNOWLEDGMENTS

General thanks and credit should be given to the Western Historical Manuscripts Division of the University of Missouri Library, the Missouri Historical Society at St. Louis, and the Illinois State Historical Library at Springfield. The staff of the State Historical Society of Missouri at Columbia, especially the newspaper librarians, was also most helpful and congenial.

A small group of individuals have contributed to the completion of this study and deserve special mention. Russell Clemens should be rewarded for just being himself. He provided the ingredient of changeableness to the group, and the willingness to discuss life's larger questions in ways that were appropriately serious, cynical, and humorous. Larry Gragg read portions of the manuscript and offered helpful suggestions. He also provided the measure of solid friendship that helped throughout. Christopher Gibbs read and critically commented on the various drafts of the manuscript, and discussions with him concerning history in general helped to place the project in its proper historical perspective. As a friend and as a colleague, on a professional level in all aspects, his help has been invaluable. I hope I can return the favor. Lawrence Goodwyn provided criticisms and comments along the way that were most beneficial. He also shared a brilliant and passionate book on Populism, and provided a great deal of inspiration. The greatest debt of all I owe to David Thelen. He urged me to examine and interpret the historical process, and provided thoughtful and critical analysis of the book in all its stages. His knowledge and enthusiasm made the project more interesting and exciting, his friendship made it more meaningful. I consider myself fortunate on all counts. If a slogan can represent an endeavor, the one that has meaning here is "Five friends is an army."

The
Anti-Monopoly
Persuasion

INTRODUCTION

Between the Civil War and the First World War American society underwent a process of rapid industrialization. It was a time, as historians have chosen to call it, of the rise of big business. Entrepreneurs forged large corporations and then attempted to make them even larger to escape market insecurities. They vertically integrated their activities by expanding toward potential markets and new raw material sources, and horizontally integrated other leading producers through various forms of combination. Ultimately the dictates of mass production and mass distribution demanded managerial experts who, among other things, applied new techniques to improve efficiency. Along the way, earlier, personal, pre-industrial values and ways of living, working, and doing business yielded to the new corporate-dominated values and modes of modern, 20th century America.

This study examines this familiar process by focusing on the popular response to the most extreme form of economic concentration, the corporate monopoly or trust. The time period selected for this study (1887–1913) has been chosen because it roughly corresponded with the most drastic phase in the growth of corporate consolidations as well as with some of the most vehement popular responses to that growth. The period provides an opportunity to examine the process by which a grass roots, broadly-based movement first challenged fundamental changes in the economic system, how that movement operated in attempting to achieve its desired ends, the effects of that movement on national policymakers, and the reasons for the ultimate decline of the movement itself.

Earlier studies of economic policy during the Gilded Age-Progressive Era, and especially of antitrust policy, have focused almost exclusively on the federal level and have given primary attention to the Sherman Antitrust Act of 1890.[1] This focus has suggested that politicians initiated the response to the formation of trusts and that only policymakers, economists, and intellectuals offered any solutions to the problem. Such a focus has missed the point. Most antitrust activity began not at the national level, but rather at the state and local level. And the impetus for that activity came not from "above," but rather from the daily experiences of ordinary people "below."

People in the Midwest in the late 19th century were neither ignorant nor uninformed. They were well aware of their relationship as individuals to basic democratic principles and of important social, economic, and political issues. Such philosophical considerations were important because so many of the people of that region felt oppressed. They lived in a region caught in the rapid transformation from frontier communities to semi-industrial areas with major urban centers, where frontier democracy confronted modern industrialization. Such abrupt changes seemed to intensify the expression of a native, agrarian-industrial radicalism that arose out of a tradition of independence. This Midwestern spirit of protest was, as Russell B. Nye has described it, "simply its own, compounded out of its geography, its culture, its economic and social history."[2] The particular demands for reform of the economic system that issued forth from the Midwest during this period did not come from a narrowly defined group of enlightened liberals, articulate middle-class Americans, or a new breed of visionary businessman. Instead, the response proved to be much broader as it transcended class, particular professional role or occupation, and any exclusive agrarian-rural or industrial-labor focus. People spoke from everyday experiences and offered their own popular analysis of the impact that industrial capitalism and corporate consolidation had upon their lives.

Ever since the Declaration of Independence, Americans have possessed a guiding democratic ideology and a belief that the majority should control political power. During the Revolutionary period, Americans actively tested this ideology by reacting against economic, political, and social intimidation by England. They objected to the special privileges they saw being granted to other Englishmen, such as the trading monopoly on tea and other goods. They protested the denial of what they considered to be their own basic political right to representation in Parliament. They disapproved of being treated by Parliament as second-class citizens. Moved by a century and a half of colonial experience and by the rhetoric of the Revolution, citizens increasingly took part in politics and demanded democratic changes in the character of their own colonial governments. There was a distinct movement in the direction of having colonial legislatures controlled by a majority of the voters. Lower houses gained in influence and forced ruling elites to relinquish power and privilege. Many new state constitutions—with their Declarations of Rights and less regressive tax laws—resulted as the products of this sentiment.

Americans also possessed a very old common law tradition that prescribed proper moral behavior in an economic environment, one that suggested a strong popular antipathy to monopoly. For example, a person had a moral obligation to pay a fair wage, to charge a just price, or to produce goods that were not harmful to the community. Colonists, applying English common law to a new environment, consistantly objected to such economic excesses as engrossing, forestalling, and overcharging.[3] After the settlement of Jamestown in 1607, the Virginia Company instructed local authorities to suppress forestalling. In 1631 the House of Burgesses ordered statutes against forestalling and engrossing to be enforced in Virginia. Commissioners sent to investigate Bacon's Rebellion in 1677 again heard complaints that the engrossing of commodities had endangered the welfare of the community. And it was the same in other colonies. In 1634 the Massachusetts General Court fixed prices on the necessities of life, and in 1641 the Body of Liberties expressly prohibited monopolies. Urban areas were no different. In the late 17th century the cities of Boston, New York, and Philadelphia established open retail markets and prohibited the practice of forestalling. Intense popular feeling against speculators during the Revolution brought about renewed complaints against forestallers and engrossers of salt, sugar, flour, and other foods. Prices were fixed in Pennsylvania in 1776 and in New Jersey and Massachusetts in 1777. In June, 1779, a handbill signed "Vengeance" circulated in Boston urging citizens to call a mass meeting to drive monopolizers from the city. Many of the Declarations of Rights in the first state constitutions embodied this popular hostility to monopoly.[4] These early Americans had an inherent conception of an ideal society.

As America entered the Jacksonian era the nation appeared, on the surface, to have become noticeably more democratic. Jackson himself challenged the monopolistic Bank of the United States in the name of the people, while politicians celebrated the common man with a heavy dose of egalitarian rhetoric and raised the banner of one-white-man-one-vote. A freer, more opportunistic environment for competitive capitalism also developed for the small entrepreneur. But certain anti-democratic tendencies had arisen and complaints of injustices abounded. Labor leaders and reformers described a society marked by increasing poverty and misery, highlighted by a class of idle rich in stark contrast to an ever-more-present class of laboring poor. These leaders realized that wealth, especially new economic wealth, had the potential to control political power, exacerbate social distinctions, and destroy economic opportunity.

Just as the hope of witnessing the realization of the democratic dream loomed largest for some, the pace of economic growth began to destroy the dream itself for many others. More and more men and women went to work in mills and factories, and mill and factory owners sought to control and discipline their employees in order to increase productivity and maximize profits. Many workers felt that they, by their labor, gave all value to the goods they produced, but received little economic benefit from the sale of those goods. The factory system had endangered the right of men and women to enjoy the fruits of their labors and talents. Slowly, many of the producing segments within society began to feel that their inalienable rights had been taken from them. This sentiment surfaced in 1835 in the short-lived Equal Rights Party, more commonly known under the sobriquet of "Loco-Foco." Centered in New York City, this party formulated a conception of democracy that espoused the philosophy of human equality in a Christian context. Proclaiming their mission to be a return to the principles of the Declaration of Independence—"those heaven-born principles . . . trodden under foot of Monopoly"—Loco-Focos assailed chartered corporations and used common law rhetoric against the new corporate "forestallers" and "engrossers."[5] Their awareness of what democracy meant increased by their being deprived of a portion of the rights that they thought democracy guaranteed.

Chester McArthur Destler has suggested that by 1865 in the upper Mississippi Valley a system of democratic thought had developed, derived from a blend of native "coonskin democracy" and the transplanted "urban radicalism" of the earlier Loco-Foco program. The resulting political environment included an insistence upon equal rights and an intense hostility to monopoly, usually directed at banks and chartered corporations. Destler also found that people continued to place great emphasis on the tradition of natural rights and the idea of a social compact.[6]

For almost half a century following the Civil War various popular reform movements, especially in the Midwest, sought to determine the course of the changing political economy. Characteristically, each expression of democratic protest, in its own particular way, was out of step with rising industrial capitalism. In the 1870s the Patrons of Husbandry instituted an organized response to the monopolistic practices of the new railroads, and sought to convince lawmakers of the need to regulate their marketing and rate-making operations. Local granges also attempted various cooperative experiments to circumvent the exactions of middlemen and manufacturers. Cooperatives improved purchasing and marketing strength, thereby removing credit restraints from some and restoring economic opportunity to others. During the 1880s the Agricultural Wheel and the Farmers' Alliance built upon Granger beginnings and actively challenged the new economic order. These reform organizations detested the impositions of banking and manufacturing monopolies in credit and prices, and railed at the exactions of middlemen and merchants who kept them in bondage through "anaconda" mortgages on their crops, farm stock, and land. As a means of regaining their economic independence, the Wheel

and Alliance experimented with cooperative trading, marketing, and manufacturing pursuits. These two organizations,
united by the thread of anti-monopoly, used both their numer-
ical strength and democratic aspirations to influence (and then
challenge) the major political parties, and pushed for the first
antitrust laws as a means of restoring their basic democratic
freedoms.

As the nation grew industrially, other groups became more
acutely aware of the loss of their economic independence. The
factory system brought with it an industrial discipline, a modernizing technology, and a time-orientation that undermined
older pre-industrial values, work habits, and task-oriented styles
of work.[7] Whistles and time clocks governed the workplace, and
workers increasingly found themselves relegated to mere cogs
in an impersonal industrial system. New conditions of dependence eroded the pride in one's skill and the satisfaction in
creating a "finished" product, the sense of "manhood," independence, and respect gained as the owner of one's tools, and
the security of being able to provide for a family. Many workingmen discovered that control over the nature of the workplace was, as David Montgomery has suggested, extremely important for preserving the endangered autonomy, work rules,
and brotherhood of craftsmen.[8]

Urban consumers confronted changes that were no less "real."
The growth of industrial capitalism had destroyed traditional
relationships among groups in society. In a pre-industrial society, artisans and consumers very often knew each other and
conducted business on a face-to-face level. These personal en-
counters provided consumers with a means by which to control producers, while community traditions and public regulations helped to govern price and product quality in a traditional
manner. As agricultural and manufacturing markets developed, middlemen and employers intervened to disrupt this
process and alienated production from consumption. Soon,
monopolies, with their control over manufacturing and marketing, formally curtailed the direct, independent interaction that
had once brought people together. In such an impersonal environment there seemed to be no avenue of redress for complaint, no one to assume ultimate responsibility. Industrial cap-

italism also brought with it polluted water and air, adulterated food, and inefficient and unsafe services. Consumers found that control over product quality, safety and price were vital economic and moral concerns.

Small retailers and small producers found that they had something in common with workers and consumers. They tended to define economic independence in two ways. The opportunity to compete equally in the marketplace was important, but so, too, was the desire to control one's own business. However, the rapidly changing economic system restricted the chances of turning a profit and exercising independent control in a free market. Small businessmen and "independent" producers found it increasingly difficult to compete in a market dominated by great combinations of industry and transportation. Control over inventories, prices, and one's security had been assumed by others.

The movement to reform the economic system and restore democracy coalesced in the 1890s as social tensions unified these diverse groups. The depression of the 1890s intensified the popular feeling of economic oppression and broadened the popular base of discontent. The depression caused people to reflect upon the past "advances" of industrialization, heightened their social awareness as citizens, and caused them to scrutinize personal relationships in an increasingly impersonal society. Unemployment, tax inequities, and inadequate municipal services further fueled a rising civic indignation. Hard times and the common feelings of doubt and anger brought people together. They sensed a new interdependence and began to generate a new spirit of resistance to the social, political, and economic implications of the process of large-scale industrial capitalism. The exposés of reform journalists and the speeches and actions of reform-minded public servants helped to focus this resistance. The result was a fusion of feeling, thought, and commitment to action.[9]

By the turn of the century the pervasiveness of trust control over the ways of living, working, and doing business reminded consumers, workers, and small retailers that they were natural allies against a common enemy. Utilizing the boycott, they discovered both a way to discipline trusts and a means of mutual support.[10] They also hoped that anti-monopoly laws would help them. Aggressive enforcement of state antitrust laws was one tactic. Courts levied strict fines, revoked corporate charters, and threatened corporate directors with imprisonment as a means of disciplining corporations. As the elimination of economic injustice was paramount, the public justified boycotts, strikes, seizures, and condemnations from pulpit, bench, and press. These anti-monopolists reacted democratically to what they perceived to be special privilege and imposition from a dominant class from above, its position made secure by its wealth and by its control of political and economic power. They adopted the concept of "public interest" as a standard by which to judge the corporation, and believed that their efforts could restore economic independence and revitalize democracy in American society. But the forces of large-scale industrial capitalism proved to be too strong, and the methods of economic and political cooptation too effective. The dream of an independent, moral economy was replaced with the reality of a modern, controlled, amoral economy based on unlimited economic growth and profit maximization. The values of economic elites, in direct opposition to democratic values, triumphed.

ROOTS TO REACTION: **1**
THE POPULAR ORIGINS OF
THE ANTITRUST
MOVEMENT

The rapid growth of industrial capitalism following the Civil War had a tremendous impact upon all aspects of American society. In a manner, it hastened the transition from the old, traditional, pre-industrial society to the new, modern, industrial order. Large-scale forms of corporate organization and nation-wide mass-market and mass-production operations characterized the new norm. These developments had the effect of creating new attitudes toward the economic process itself and toward those social relationships that were being subordinated to the emerging order of things. Many people welcomed the changes, regarding them as "modern," but the enthusiasm of some within that group quickly waned as they discovered their own economic opportunities were narrowing. Others regarded the changes in a more "traditional" manner. To them, the goal was preservation. They began thinking about ways of living that had worked in the past but were suddenly incompatible with the new industrial order. They remembered a more personalized existence, when farmers produced for consumption or for sale in a local market, when workers knew employers and producers very often knew consumers, when people set their own pace and hours of work and regarded themselves as craftsmen of various sorts, and when consumers felt reasonably secure with the prices charged and confident of the quality of the goods produced. If the old ways were, perhaps, not quite so idyllic as some remembered, one thing all could agree on—the growth of the new ways was a very anti-democratic process. The problem was, what should be done about it?

The first step was to pay close attention to the ways the new system worked, so one had a chance to analyze where things had gone wrong. It was rather apparent, for instance, that certain forces had moved into a dominant position. Some of these forces seemed to have exclusive control over certain commodities, for example.[1] It was also evident that wealth was rapidly accumulating in the hands of a few. Debtors saw the exorbitant interest charges exacted by money-lenders as the cause and they traced it to the usurious banking and credit system that seemed to have developed. Not only wealth but the land itself seemed to be caught in some centralizing system. In the 1865–1885 period people began to speak of "land monopolies" as well as the "money trust." There were many dimensions to both. Speculators and railroads preempted free land and forced the price up.

Akin to this second monopoly, and financially controlled and managed by the first, was a third major source of monopoly activity—the railroad. To the farmer slowly entering the market economy, prosperity depended upon the distribution network for the sale of his products and for the purchase of his goods. Accordingly, farmers sought inexpensive transportation rates and an end to discriminating hauling charges and rebates. They wanted reduced costs in the handling of commodities by middlemen, and the political influence of the railroad lobby curbed. In these various ways, then, the three broad monopolies of banking, land ownership, and transportation, together with the related problems of credit, currency, mortgages, crop liens, taxes, bonds, rates, prices, and political influence all came to dominate the attention of much of American society in the generation after the Civil War.

People who thought about these sundry economic happenings gradually acquired a name for themselves. They were "anti-monopolists." The label covered a multitude of urges and longings. It applied to those who resisted the process of monopolization itself, the ever-increasing size and numbers of economic concentrations and the exclusiveness of control over goods and services. And those who worried about the implications of the monopolistic trend—the elimination of competition, economic opportunity, and authentic republican government—were also called anti-monopolists. Their ranks included people of many tendencies. While it is probably fair to describe some of them as "disaffected modernists" and others as "nostalgic traditionalists," they shared a common presumption: they did not like the tilt of the "new" America. Who were they? They were mainly producer-oriented groups of farmers, workers, or merchants. Though they were united in the common belief that their economic independence had been stolen, their perceptions of that independence differed. Some basically accepted the economic system and longed for the continued opportunity to compete equally in it. Others tended to reject the new conditions that had turned them into either wage slaves or debtors, and they sought to return economic circumstances to an earlier time. Both groups had a common enemy, monopoly, and for twenty years their anti-monopoly movement sought solutions within a dominant producer-oriented framework.

The struggle that took place in the late 19th century between agrarian elements and the railroad provides a rather clear view of how exclusive control over commodities and services operated, and how both modern and traditional anti-monopolists responded to the effects of that operation. When towns or counties sold bonds to attract the railroads, the taxes of farmers were increased to pay off the bonds. Many Western communities suffered under this heavy tax burden. Public indebtedness was such a problem in Kansas during the 1880s that estimates placed the portion of the state's municipal debt incurred to help subsidize the railroads at 80 percent. Market-oriented farmers—along with Midwestern merchants, Eastern import and shipping interests, and independent Pennsylvania oil producers—suffered from the railroad rate-fixing structure and discriminations. To make matters worse, they rarely had a choice of railroad companies with which to deal. Railroads not only reached agreements among themselves, they also consolidated their lines. This centralizing process was quite rapid. According to one Minnesota railway commissioner: "The number of separate railroad companies operating distinct roads in Minnesota was as high as twenty, three years ago. Now the number is reduced to substantially one-third that number."[2] Older lines often bought out parallel or competing lines and obtained absolute control.[3]

The farmer also had no control over the prices of commodi-

ties purchased by him as a consumer. It was clear to him that
the trusts had joined with the railroads and had bribed politicians "to hold the people's hands and pick their pockets."[4]
Middlemen or monopolistic manufacturers fixed the price of all
goods either sold or purchased by the farmer. These middlemen, as the agents who handled articles on a commission basis
from the manufacturer, were of two types—commission merchants and produce dealers who bought, and the retail merchants who sold. When crop prices fell, farmers blamed the
commission merchants for fixing prices, singly or in combination. When profits disappeared, farmers blamed exorbitant
commission rates and the "toll-taking hands" of the commission agents. When retail prices became excessive, farmers blamed
the retail merchant or his master, the manufacturer.[5]

The farmer also had to contend with the credit-banking monopoly. Farmers generally lacked ready cash and were forced
to buy on credit. This was especially true in the South where
"furnishing merchants," who received goods on consignment
from Northern commission houses, "furnished" the same goods
to farmers in exchange for a lien on the farmer's crop as security. But the problems of the Southern farmer had only just
started. Unable to pay his current debt, he was forced to mortgage his next year's crop to the merchant. Studies by the Georgia Department of Agriculture (1881–1889) and the Louisiana
State Bureau of Agriculture (1886–1896) show that the furnishing merchant exacted interest rates often in excess of 60 percent. The merchant further burdened the farmer by placing him
on a two-price system with higher prices for credit than for cash
customers. In the West, farmers who had recently moved to the
frontier often needed money to finance improvements or to fight
through hard times. Mortgage companies, backed by Eastern
capital, responded to the demand. Money was easily extended,
and, in many cases, overextended. Farmers borrowed heavily
and the per capita mortgage debt in the West was extremely
high.[6] Then, in the late 1880s, the bottom dropped out in both
regions. Cotton prices fell in the South, and, in 1887, drought
struck the West. Farmers in both regions faced an insurmount-
able burden of debt.[7]

Economic grievances aroused the farmer to action, and his

initial response was to turn to voluntary, cooperative organizations to promote his welfare and to combat monopoly. The earliest of such organizations was the Patrons of Husbandry started in 1867 by Oliver H. Kelley. With a legion of local "granges," and a strong anti-railroad focus, the Order flourished during the 1870s. Kelley, himself, did not seem startled by the success as he remarked in 1871 that " 'Cooperation' and 'Down with monopolies' were providing popular watchwords."[8] During the 1870s the states of Illinois, Minnesota, Wisconsin, and Iowa passed important regulatory measures to establish state control over railroads. Though the sponsorship of the so-called "Granger laws" has been vigorously debated by historians, organized farmers certainly showed their support for legislation to curb a major monopoly. Grangers, along with other interests, pressured their state legislatures to establish controlling agencies such as the boards of railroad commissioners, and managed to see new railroad laws enacted. The new laws established schedules of maximum rates, included "short haul" clauses to prevent discriminations, levied taxes on railroad property, and attempted to preserve competition by forbidding the consolidation of parallel lines.[9]

As an example of success in one other state, the Missouri State Grange, representing some 2,000 local granges and 100,000 farmers, declared for railroad regulation in October of 1874. The following year the influence of the Grange, and of certain "Confederate" elements in the state who hoped to curb the excessive freedoms and tax exemptions that "Unionists" were eager to grant railroads and corporations, forced the inclusion of Article 12 in the Missouri State Constitution. This provision gave the legislature the apparent power to regulate railroads as it established a Board of Railroad Commissioners, provided that freight rates be determined on a pound-distance basis, and levied a tax on railroad property. In practice, however, the results were meager. The Board of Railroad Commissioners merely served as an advisory body, having no authority to bring suit against any railroad.[10]

States might control and regulate the charges and rates of the railroads that ran through them, but they could do little to combat the exactions of distant buyers, middlemen, and manufacturers. Grangers were aware that any successes depended upon collective action. The solution that was compatible with their means and hopefully productive of the end result of economic independence was the cooperative experiment. Producer cooperatives could circumvent middlemen and manufacturers, while the collective strength of the cooperative could drive a better bargain in the marketplace. Consumer cooperatives could provide that same bargaining or, in this case, purchasing strength, while eliminating the middleman, manufacturing agent, or retail merchant. The restoration of economic opportunity would greet some, while others would be freed from debt or rigid credit restraints. Grangers, as producers, could look to increased profits, and, as consumers, they could expect lower prices. All participants would regain a degree of personal control over what had become an impersonal economic system.

The various granges undertook a variety of cooperative schemes such as purchasing, marketing, and manufacturing to battle the price-fixing influence of middlemen and monopolistic manufacturers. One of the earliest schemes took place in Chicago in 1873 when the Northwestern Farmer's Convention adopted resolutions that recommended that farmers withhold hogs from the market until price levels stabilized. Later, numerous county and subordinate groups in Illinois and other Midwestern states made similar attempts. Local, county, and state grange cooperative agencies were formed in Iowa, Illinois, Kansas, Nebraska, and Missouri. At the National Grange Convention in 1874 members were urged to work together, buy together, and sell together. Purchasing and marketing agents located in the major retail centers to perform cooperative buying and selling functions. When the exactions of the "Harvester Ring" and the "Plow Ring" continued to be problems, the granges attempted the cooperative manufacture of harvesters, plows, wagons, sewing machines, and threshers. But most undertakings proved unsuccessful. Other factories such as grist mills, cheese and butter factories, linseed oil factories, pork-packing plants, hemp factories, and cotton mills were either projected or actually established. These various ventures showed the earliest organized attempts by farmers to regain their economic independence from middlemen and monopolists, be they capitalists, bankers, merchants, or manufacturers.[11]

During the 1880s, as farm conditions worsened, two new agrarian organizations, known as the Wheel and Alliance, arose to take the place of the Grange. The Agricultural Wheel was first organized in Prairie County, Arkansas, in February, 1882, by a small gathering of farmers who had formed a debating group. The debates were directed mainly against political corruption and monopoly.[12] The Wheel soon moved from political rhetoric to economic cooperation and the Wheel cooperatives proved a great boon to recruitment. By 1887 the Wheel had extended into eight states and numbered perhaps 200,000 members. W. W. Tedford, one of the earliest "wheelers," remarked: "The question has often been asked, what gave rise to the Wheel? This question is as easily answered as asked, monopoly! A monopoly that wants to buy the earth, and with it the souls and bodies of the people who inhabit it."[13] Members of the Wheel spoke of trusts and combines but complained most about the monopoly in business and the "anaconda" mortgages which furnishing merchants obtained on crops, farm stock, and land. As was the case throughout the South, merchants "held" these mortgages by charging usurious prices for the goods they furnished. Once a farmer signed a mortgage, he became practically the slave of the mortgage holder. The mortgagee deprived the farmer of other means of credit and compelled the farmer to trade only with him. Wheel cooperatives were designed to circumvent this web of dependency. Building upon its mass base in the coops, the Wheel moved into politics in an effort to obtain additional economic progress through legislation. Consistent with its anti-monopoly position, the Wheel denied membership to those engaged in law, banking, manufacturing, speculating, railroads, insurance, and stores other than of the cooperative variety. This anti-monopoly base of the Wheel, grounded in the order's cooperatives which were described as a "grand and distinctive feature of the Order," placed it firmly within the anti-monopoly tradition and made it easily compatible with the Farmers' Alliance that swept out of the South to join it in the 1880s.[14]

The Alliance also stressed the idea of cooperation as a means of improving the farmer's economic condition and as a way of resisting the grip of middlemen and monopoly. One Erath County (Texas) Alliance Cooperative official boasted that: "We can purchase anything we want through our agent, dry goods, and groceries, farm implements and machinery."[15] Cooperative stores, elevators, gins, mutual marketing, and insurance and purchasing agencies all formed a part of the Alliance program. To break away from the furnishing merchant, farmers rushed to join the Alliance and form cooperative trade stores in the mid–1880s. They also sought relief from the excessive charges levied by the trusts on fertilizer and farm implements by forming cooperative buying committees.[16]

Farmer grievances increased during the drought-stricken days of the late eighties. In California, Missouri, an Alliance daily, simply called *The Newspaper*, continued to attack the perennial problem of the land monopoly and its impact upon public indebtedness. Farmers resented paying the interest and principal on debts incurred in the construction of the railroads. Speaking to farmers everywhere, *The Newspaper* referred to census data to produce figures of the total land under cultivation in the United States. Added to these statistics was the estimated "watered debt" of the railroads on lands in excess of actual cost. The editor's calculations yielded figures that showed that every farmer was burdened by an 8 percent railroad corporation mortgage (equal to $20) on each and every acre he tilled. Said the editors: "There is a $20 an acre railroad mortgage on every one of your farms. There is a $10 public debt mortgage on every acre you till. There is a $10 bank and money power mortgage on each improved acre, and you can't sell your farms to-day for sufficient to clear off these blood-sucking vampires."[17]

The rural press persistently attacked other problems that continued to beset the farmer. The editors of the *Tipton Times* (Missouri) focused on the railroad monopoly and felt compelled to comment: "Year after year the railroads have extorted exorbitant rates from our people for all sorts of traffic; the most shameless discriminations have been practiced; our plain statute laws have been ignored and set at defiance, until the masses are indignant and rightly so."[18] To the *Nebraska State Journal*, the problem was tight credit and that "old sign we all of us used to see hanging in a prominent place in every country store, 'No Trust,' has lately acquired a deeper and broader significance than ever before."[19] A cartoon in the *St. Louis Republican* in March,

1888, showed an Eastern capitalist leading a line of chained and handcuffed farmers into a courthouse upon which was a sign which read "Farm Mortgages Foreclosed Here."[20] One Missouri editor, angered over the exactions of the "plow trust," remarked that: "As soon as it [trust] was perfected the price of plows went up 100 percent . . . who suffers? Who, indeed, but the farmer?" Iowans denounced the "beef trust," Kansans complained of a "produce trust," and Southern farmers villified the "fertilizer trust," the "jute bagging trust," and the "cottonseed oil trust."[21] The historian of the Wheel and Alliance adequately summed up the farmer's plight when he stated: "Trusts, syndicates and combinations demand extortion on everything we buy; and transportation companies, pools and middlemen levy tribute on everything we sell."[22] To the farmer, his farm products as well as his food, fuel, and clothing were all controlled by someone else.

The intensity of the popular response to monopoly seemed to relate directly to the drastic increase in the number of industrial combinations formed after 1887—the year, ironically enough, when the Interstate Commerce Commission was formed to regulate railroads. Where only six industrial consolidations had taken place during the entire period from 1860–1886, eight occurred in the year 1887 alone. By 1890 the number of trusts had soared to forty-two.[23]

In the summer of 1888 the price of jute bagging doubled from 7 cents to 14 cents a yard, because of the formation of a St. Louis-based trust, and farmers in the cotton belt decided to fight back. Members of the Texas State Farmers' Alliance had undertaken efforts at cooperative marketing in 1886, when they attempted to "bulk" their cotton to lure competitive buyers to the marketplace. But when prices soared the following year Southern cotton farmers in Alabama, Tennessee, Georgia, Louisiana, Mississippi, Florida, and North and South Carolina held meetings to protest the increases and to boycott jute. Farmers began to wrap their cotton bales in pine straw and coarse cotton cloth substitutes and to recycle old jute bags. This increased both the demand and price of old bags, but the growers chose to buy the old jute bags rather than deal from the trust. The Mississippi State Alliance considered plans for a bagging factory to be set up within the state penitentiary at Jackson and run by prison labor. In Georgia, 200 delegates of the State Alliance passed a resolution which stated that they would use only cotton bagging. The Alabama Alliance passed a similar resolution and actually purchased a site for a cotton bagging factory. At a Georgia Alliance convention, held during the "jute war," one farmer came dressed up in cotton bagging and told of 360 alliancemen in his county who had uniforms made from the same material and were known as the "cotton bagging brigade." And in Bonham, Texas, a typical mass meeting of farmers was held and circulars were printed and distributed throughout the county to rally support. By 1890 enough cotton bagging had been substituted for jute that jute bagging was selling as low as 5 cents a yard.[24]

The problems that confronted Southern farmers in their dealings with the jute bagging trust resembled closely those that faced farmers on the Great Plains over the binding twine trust in the spring of 1889. When the price of binding twine increased from 9 cents to 25 cents per pound, Midwestern farmers who needed to bind their wheat felt exploited. It seemed that they were being forced to pay a monstrous "tax" to save their crops. Wheat farmers resisted this imposition and responded as the Southern cotton farmers had. They boycotted binding twine and signed petitions that pledged them to stack their grain without binding. Examples of support for these actions were numerous. Farmers in Brown County, Kansas, met to protest the increase in the price of agricultural supplies, "the extortions of the binding twine trust." Following the meeting the county alliance took action to establish a cooperative binding twine factory. The farmers of McLean County, Illinois, joined in the crusade against the trust. They held a convention and adopted resolutions that pledged all those present not to use twine in the coming harvest unless the price was reduced. In Missouri a "largely attended" meeting of farmers, under the direction of the Audrain County Wheel, took place in the town of Mexico to consider the best means of confronting the trust. The participants adopted a statement by which they agreed not to purchase twine at the existing exorbitant prices proposed by the trust, "or at any other unreasonable price." In April, 1889, a resolution was introduced in the Illinois legislature, much like the earlier action taken in Mississippi, which directed the Commissioner of Penitentiaries to investigate the cost of operating a prison-run binding twine factory as a means of instilling competition. Farmers also made at least one attempt to unite action on a regional level. Alliance leaders in Minnesota, Dakota, Iowa, Nebraska, Kansas, and Missouri agreed to meet to perfect an organization for the purpose of breaking down the existing twine trust.[25]

The real success and importance of the responses to both the jute bagging and binding twine trusts lay in the publicity, exposure, and discussion that resulted. Trusts had become the topic of concern. The strength of local animosities had begun to apply pressure at the state, regional, and national levels. Farmers realized the implications of trust formation and associated their economic difficulties with the spread of industrial combinations. When the Pomona Grange of Navarro County, Texas, petitioned Congress in 1889, they prayed for the passage of a law to relieve their county from the effects of all trusts. When the Tiff City Farmers' Alliance of McDonald County, Missouri, petitioned Congress, it was to urge them to vote for all bills that would kill "all trusts and moneyed combinations."[26]

In the late 1880s the character of the anti-monopoly movement changed. The growth of the city in both physical size and in the numbers of people who lived there necessitated a tremendous expansion in the goods and services required by consumers. To promote the expansion of municipal services, cities granted exclusive franchises to street railways, illuminating gas, and electric lighting companies. In return for the privileges granted by the franchise, urban consumers expected to be charged a fair price and to receive safe and efficient operation of service. This same "understanding" or "civic contract" carried over to the retail sale of goods such as food, coal, and ice. Consumers naturally expected to pay a "just" price. Accepting slight price fluctuations as due to the forces of supply and demand, consumers, nevertheless, expected the free operation of competition to keep those fluctuations "reasonable." They soon discovered, however, that trusts forced people of all classes to buy trust goods at trust prices, and gave no guarantees of quality or cost. Consumers quickly gained an understanding of what exclusive control over commodities and services could mean on a personal level that farmers already possessed. Whether they were private individuals or small businessmen, urban consumers felt the loss of their own economic independence. As consumers joined the sufferers, they also joined the ranks of the anti-monopolists. Borrowing the worker-farmer tools of protest, cooperation, and boycott against the emerging system of large-scale industrial capitalism, consumers joined with producers in support of legislation to attack the problem of monopoly. The first state antitrust laws were to materialize from their efforts.

One example of the way consumers responded to trust price imposition occurred in St. Louis in 1887. In the spring of that year the Retail Ice Dealers' Association sent out circulars to consumers informing them of a probable shortage of ice in the St. Louis area. As a result, ice would have to be shipped in by railroad at advanced rates. But consumers, led by small retailers who needed lots of ice, denied the reports of shortages and accused the "ice pool" of attempting to corner the market. William F. Frazer, a confectioner, felt that there was a plentiful supply and that it was robbery to demand 45 cents per hundred pounds when ice could be sold at a profit for 25 cents. William A. Addington, a druggist, agreed and stated that he was taking ice from an "outsider" and getting it at 25 cents, while the pool wanted 50 cents. He said that he had been threatened by the pool and would be charged $1 per hundred if his current dealer failed. The pool attempted to frighten other customers of independent distributors by telling them that independents would run out of ice and that consumers would be forced to buy ice from the pool at increased prices. William V. Miller, a local distributor, felt such pressure, but stated that he could bring in ice from Chicago and sell it at 25 cents and make a profit. To the populace, it appeared as if they were being forced to pay a double price for a necessary item. As one editor stated: "Ice is not a luxury in this climate, but a necessity, and the attempt to extort big profits on it is almost as bad as extortion on bread. It means untold increase in the suffering of the poor, and on children, whose food depends often on being kept cool. The hardship also on the sick poor is inestimable."[27] One poor woman had received her ice from the pool and owed a bill there. The pool wrote her a letter stating that if her bill was not immediately paid, her name would be inserted into the "black book," and she would be unable to obtain a pound of ice during the summer. The pool used this "black book" as a threat to compel consumers to buy pool ice at pool prices.[28]

The ice pool made two mistakes. It overestimated the completeness of the combine, and it underestimated the willingness of consumers to resort to the boycott. Ice was available from other dealers in and around St. Louis. Supplies could be brought in from a distance of 300 miles and sold for a profit at little more than half the pool price. Consumers could also act on their own. When the pool made war on Holahan and O'Brien, an independent dealership that sold ice at from 20 to 40 cents a hundred, their customers refused to bolt even when the pool offered to sell ice at 10 cents. The St. Louis Butchers' Union agreed not to deal with "association" men. And the inhabitants of Chestnut Street wrote a letter to the *St. Louis Post-Dispatch* and invited any agent of an anti-pool dealer to canvass their neighborhood. Anti-pool dealers took the hint and sent their names and addresses to the newspaper so that consumers could have a choice. Citizens held a protest meeting at Central Turner Hall and issued a statement that "if ever there was an unholy alliance of monopoly to squeeze blood-money out of the public on a necessity of life this is one of them."[29] At the consumption rate of 1886, the *Post-Dispatch* calculated that pool price increases would mean $1,000,000 more to the consumers of St. Louis. When, in defiance of public opinion, the combine adopted a brass star as the symbol of their association, and vowed to place it on all of their wagons, the same newspaper referred to the star as the "brand of extortion." Citizens had hoped to break up the ice pool, or, "in the words of John L. Sullivan, do them up," and they were successful. On June 6, 1887, after two months of fighting, the ice combine reduced all prices.[30]

Urban consumers felt the effects of trust consolidation in other municipal services as well. The encounter with the Ice Trust showed consumer indignation at what was perceived as price imposition on the part of a trust or pool. However, consumers could also show contempt for the quality of service as revealed in their dealings with the St. Louis Gas Trust. In July of 1887, a joint committee of the St. Louis Council and House of Delegates responded to a general consumer complaint over poor gas service, and made arrangements to begin an investigation of possible pooling on the part of several illuminating gas companies. The so-called Gas Trust first appeared in the spring of 1886 when the St. Louis Gaslight Company joined with a Philadelphia group which controlled the rival St. Louis Gas, Fuel, and Power Company. Prohibitions against direct amalgamation and pooling in the charter of the company forced the new partners to accept a modified version of the trust form of agreement first used by the Standard Oil Company. A group of trustees had the physical plants of the companies assessed, the value of the stock estimated, and then took control over the value of the stock. When questioned by the *Post-Dispatch* about the arrangement, President W. H. Thompson of the Gas Trust remarked: "There is no law to prevent you and me from pooling our earnings or our interests if we want to; and there is no law to prevent our appointing a trustee to look out after our joint interests."[31]

Consumer complaints regarding the operation of such an essential municipal service persisted into the fall of 1887. The existing charters protected the public through the inclusion of price ceilings that prevented the gas companies from charging more than $1.50 per thousand feet of gas until the year 1890. In addition to this, a municipally employed gas expert was to make regular "candle power" tests of the quality of illuminating gas furnished to the city. But the quality of service was unacceptable to many consumers. Alex Mastbrook, a druggist, complained that he could not get any light: "The gas burns without life and no brilliance; it is smoky and smells very bad."[32] Mr. Mastbrook was only one of many. Fruit dealers, clothing companies, hotels, cigar merchants, haberdashers, and jewelers all filed similar complaints. The *Post-Dispatch* did some research and found that a comparison of the figures for gas consumption in the city's public buildings for the periods 1885–1886 and 1887–1888 showed a 37 percent increase. Comptroller Robert A. Campbell was asked to explain the increased consumption. Had new offices opened? Had the hours of business changed? His answer was no, and he stated: "No new offices have been created, and no change has been made in the hours of office duty. The city, like any other consumer, has the worst of it. The consumer must stand by the meter showing unless you can prove its inaccuracy, and even if you do prove it inaccurate today that is no proof that it was inaccurate three months ago."[33] The *Post-Dispatch* also discovered that though the city paid the gas "expert" $1,000 a year to make daily tests, only "half a dozen" tests had been made in nearly two years. The gas expert did not even know what candle power the ordinance required. The City Council faced a doubly complex problem. Consumers had asked them to examine the quality of gas in the city, but their examination forced them into their first confrontation with the new trust form of municipal consolidation. They were able to respond to the first problem, but could only defer any solutions to the second.[34]

The complaints of consumers and the exposures of the *Post-Dispatch* pressed the City Council and House of Delegates to take some action. When the joint committee finally did present the report of their inquiry on May 19, 1888, they recommended that the city light the streets, public places, and public buildings with electricity—the first step in the removal of public lighting from the gas interests. The committee also advised that the city conduct, control, and maintain a gas works to supply the general public with gas for illuminating, heating, domestic, mechanical, and other purposes. The city could thus regain control of the situation. Prices to consumers could be reduced, the quality of service improved, city revenues increased for public improvements or for a reduction in the general tax rate, and the burden of a trust removed. A year later the St. Louis Board of Public Improvements responded to the revised ordinance, whereby the city would be lighted by electricity, and awarded the new contracts.[35]

The consumers in St. Louis had shown that they were aware of the influence of monopolization upon aspects of their daily lives, and that they had a general understanding of the term trust (although its confusion with the term pool has been noted). But even though consumer actions had resisted the exorbitant price increases of, and had rejected an inadequate quality of service performed by, the trusts, the legal entity of the "trust agreement" had gone unchallenged. Both producers and consumers could express themselves as vigorous anti-monopolists, but consumers had only begun to feel the effects of consolidation. Producers, on the other hand, were far more organized, and the economic hardships they had continually faced as a result of land, transportation, and banking and credit monopolies were compounded in the late 1880s by the spread of various manufacturing combines. If a legislative challenge was to come then, it seemed only reasonable that producers would be the ones to lead it.

The first united effort among state policymakers to deal with the problem of trusts derived from a popular revolt against Chicago's beef combine of Armour, Swift, and Morris. On September 10, 1888, the *St. Louis Post-Dispatch* carried a seemingly bizarre story from the *Chicago Times* that a gigantic beef trust was being secretly organized. The newspaper alleged that the American Meat Company had been organized by Eastern and foreign capitalists with a capital of $25,000,000. According to the account, the object of the company was to raise cattle, slaughter them, transport the meat to market, and then sell it through wholesale and retail outlets. The control of slaughter houses, refrigerators, and railways would all be part of the master plan. Stories such as this could only have increased the paranoia of cattle raisers who were already suffering from declining stock prices, and of consumers anticipating increases in the prices of beef products.[36]

Stockgrowers felt a deep distrust for the alleged combine. In their minds the trust had eliminated competition and was responsible for the depressed meat market. Their combined power allowed them to exert an effective influence in centralizing the meat market under their control in Kansas City and Chicago. By February the situation had grown severe enough for the Kansas legislature to undertake an investigation of the beef industry.[37] In addition to this, Governor Lyman U. Humphrey of Kansas issued a call to states in the Mississippi Valley region requesting that they send representatives to a regional convention to frame and enact uniform legislation to suppress trusts.

The Missouri legislature quickly appointed a joint Senate and House committee to select representatives to attend the convention, and passed a resolution warning that trusts crowded out healthy competition and threatened republican institutions. The resolution also stated that "stock producers, as well as the consumers of beef and pork, believe that they are suffering from the suppression and greed of an alleged beef and pork combine or trust."[38] Governor Humphrey received favorable responses from at least a dozen other states, an indication of the depth of anti-monopoly sentiment.[39]

On March 12, 1889, the delegates from at least ten states met at the Southern Hotel in St. Louis to discuss the problem of trusts and, hopefully, curb the dressed beef monopoly.[40] Though the interests of stock raisers seemed to dominate the convention, some representatives sought to elucidate the implications for consumers as well as producers. One Nebraska delegate remarked that the "object is not only to secure a proper return for our cattle raisers, but also to insure cheap and sound meat for the people." Some of the Texas representatives objected to the diseased quality of much of the beef sent out, and felt that both producers and consumers were robbed by the combine. The Texans reported that beef was higher than it was five or ten years before, while the price of cattle on the hoof had dropped considerably—to 3 to 3 1/2 cents a pound then as opposed to almost twice that amount before. In the minds of many this was a well-laid plan to raise beef prices gradually, while keeping down the price of cattle. Senator John M. High of Kansas made a strong speech in support of that idea as he described his version of the process that was then underway. The beef combine, through cooperation with the railroads, bought cattle on the hoof, hauled them out of the state, sent them back as dressed beef, and prevented competition wherever possible. The consumer paid the freight both ways in increased prices, and the cattle raiser accepted the smallest percentage of profit on the value of his stock.[41]

When the conference firmly settled down to business, several resolutions were considered, among which was one known as the "Texas measure." Under the general antitrust nature of the bill, a trust—defined as "any combination of capital, skill or acts by two or more persons, firms, corporations or associations of persons"—could not restrict trade, prevent competition, fix prices, or control production. The measure also included enforcement and penalty procedures. Persons could be fined from $50 to $500, and corporations might be forced to pay $50 for each day that such violations were committed or continued. The convention adopted the measure "almost without opposition" and the representatives requested that it be presented to the legislatures of the various states in attendance. With the protection of consumers in mind, and with the hopes that consumers could be brought to support the entire bill, the convention also adopted a hoof inspection clause.[42]

The conference was a major accomplishment in the antitrust movement. As a statement of aggressive action against the beef combine, which "had nearly ruined the cattle business" and had cost consumers "millions of dollars in the increased price that has been placed on dressed meats," the conference was of major importance. Perhaps even more significant was the willingness of the participants to seek cooperation, and the direction which that cooperation took. The delegates reached a new consensus—as Representative Norton Moses of Texas put it: "In the opinion of nearly all who have considered the question the only way to fight the monopoly is by State legislation." The delegates seemed to have little faith in the effective enforcement powers of the federal government, but it remained to be seen whether the states would respond to the call.[43]

Farmers exerted considerable pressure on their state legislatures during the late 1880s, either through one of the two major parties or through organized reform groups such as the Wheel and Farmers' Alliance. By the late 1880s the decline of the cooperative movement caused the Alliance to shift its focus to legislative reform and, later, political action to accomplish the same result. Aside from occasional instances of poor business judgment, the cooperative movement had encountered the unrelenting opposition of wholesalers, manufacturers, railroads, and banks, making success virtually impossible.

When the Alliance moved toward political involvement, the shift was gradual. The initial forms of Alliance political organization and action were the neighborhood anti-monopoly leagues which were first suggested in Texas in 1886. Gradually, over the next two years, the increased organizational strength of the Alliance and Wheel caused politicians to become extremely farm conscious and anti-monopoly conscious. When farmers complained of exorbitant rate charges and called for state regulation of railroads, one editor commented that any attempt to "disregard or thwart their demands will surely result in disaster to the men or party who permit it."[44] To broaden their political base and to enhance their legislative influence, the Alliance also made an attempt to lure the fading Knights of Labor organization into its ranks. Alliancemen felt that a common ground could be found under the banner of cooperation and anti-monopoly. The idea was a good one, for in the following year a committee from the National Order of the Knights of Labor met with a committee from the Farmers' Alliance and agreed to closer cooperation. The two organizations had come to realize that both the farmer and the wage laborer suffered from "unjust laws enacted in the interests of chartered corporations."[45]

On a local and personal level, the pressure of economic dependence was often enough to create just such a mutuality of interest between workers and farmers, and one that had an anti-monopoly basis. In many states, like Missouri, and in other rural environments, workers often found themselves suffering from the same "country store" monopoly that perpetuated the mortgage-debt subsistence of many poor farmers elsewhere.

During his first year in office in 1889, newly appointed Missouri State Labor Commissioner Lee Meriwether discovered that the same economic system exploited both farmers and workers. As an example, he cited the Mendota Mining Company, which withheld workingmen's wages six or eight weeks, and then paid them with pasteboard checks not redeemable in money until 1899. Formerly these checks could have been cashed one year after the date of issue. This system forced the Mendota miners to trade at the company store, where the company could charge whatever prices they pleased. In effect, the store robbed the miners of a large percentage of their wages. Meriwether also recognized that the farmers and workers were allied in their struggle against monopoly. In this instance the agency that brought them together was the "pluck-me" system. Under the pluck-me system, "when a farmer drives to a mining or lumber camp with his wagon of supplies, he has but one customer. The hundreds of men in the camp have no money; they cannot buy, and so it is the farmer [who] is forced to sell his produce for what the pluck-me store is willing to pay."[46] Both groups were unhappy victims of monopoly. As State Labor Commissioner, Meriwether "found this vicious system in full swing, resulting not only in strikes, but also in riots and even in several midnight murders."[47] The visions of cooperation between workers and farmers at the national level within the Farmers' Alliance, and the common grievances felt by many workers and farmers at the state and local levels, provided the Alliance with a potential reservoir of popular support for political action. Though the Alliance had stopped short of any formal third-party pronouncement in 1889, it represented a popular force whose economic grievances and anti-monopoly demands would have to be listened to by the major political parties.

When the Missouri legislature convened during the late winter and early spring of 1889, it seemed a propitious time for some legislative measure that might restrict pools, trusts, combinations, and monopolies. In response to the rising popular clamor, both major parties had vague anti-monopoly planks in their party platforms in 1888. The Democratic party condemned all trusts and monopolies, and favored "such wise legislation as will secure to both producers and consumers prices based on the laws of supply and demand."[48] The Republican party was equally aware of the vitality of the issue and proclaimed that "monopolies and trusts, oppressing the people or unfairly discriminating against local interests, are wrong in principle, and should be restrained by law."[49] The Democrats carried the election of 1888, and the occupations of the legislators of the 35th General Assembly indicated a distinct "agrarian consciousness." Nearly 40 percent of the members of the House had the word "farmer" in part or all of their occupational description, and ten of the legislators were members of the Farmers' Alliance.[50] Governor David R. Francis, ex-mayor of St. Louis and leader of the conservative commercial wing within the Democratic party, was aware of the importance of the trust question both to the people and to his party's future. He devoted a section of his inaugural address to the issue and warned Missourians of the dangers inherent in the centralizing tendencies of business: "Unchecked by any feeling of individual responsibility, moved solely by a love of gain, unfettered by the duties of citizenship, they [trusts] are enabled to perpetuate themselves by the adoption of methods and the use of agents which scruple at no means to accomplish their ends."[51]

In such a climate an antitrust bill was introduced into the Missouri legislature in January of 1889.[52] The urgings of the governor, the formal statements of endorsement from the major parties, popular support, and the recommendations of the beef trust convention to the Missouri legislature in March, were pressures enough for the passage of the law. By May 4, 1889, the House by a vote of 99 to 1, and the Senate by a vote of 21 to 3, had passed Missouri's first antitrust statute. The law provided for the punishment of pools, trusts, and conspiracies, and made such an offense a misdemeanor, punishable by a fine and imprisonment.[53] The charter of any corporation found guilty of violating the provisions of the act would be dissolved.[54] By July, 1890, when Congress passed the Sherman Act, at least thirteen states had enacted statutory antitrust provisions similar to Missouri's effort in 1889. Eight other states without statutory provisions had antitrust clauses in their state constitutions.[55]

By 1890 the movement against trusts and monopolies at the state and local levels had taken major strides forward. This had been accomplished by establishing a unity of popular feeling which enabled the passage of legislative restraints against large-scale industrial consolidations. Beginning with the widespread but unorganized agrarian complaints over banking and credit, and transportation and land monopolies, farmers slowly drew together in efforts to reestablish their own economic independence. Economically they challenged the existing system and experimented with producer and consumer cooperatives. Socially they formed organizations, like the Grange, and pressured their legislatures for state control over railroads. In the 1880s, spurred by declining economic conditions, farmers improved their organizational forms of resistance through the Wheel and Alliance. They expanded and refined the organizing principles undergirding the cooperative movement and, invigorated by the large numbers of farmers they had attracted, began to consider ways to maximize their political influence. As the number of industrial combinations increased, and as urban growth intensified the need for improved municipal services, consumers began to complain along with farmers. Consumers resisted the imposition of exclusive control over goods and services and joined the movement to preserve their own economic independence. The popularity of the anti-monopoly issue among farmers, consumers, and even among many workers, made legislative action imperative by 1889. Within months the anti-monopoly movement was at legislative high-tide, but the years that followed would certainly test both the effectiveness of the new laws and the popular resolve to continue the fight against monopoly.

MISSOURI AND MONOPOLY: THE 1890s AS AN EXPERIMENT IN LAW ENFORCEMENT

2

During the 1890s, policymakers at all levels confronted the problem of monopolization and sought solutions. The legislative answer at the federal level was the Sherman Antitrust Act. State-level policymakers, however, motivated in many early cases by Populist legislative activists and later by reform-minded attorneys general and governors, ploddingly sought their own trial-and-error remedies. The importance of this second group to the continuation of the antitrust movement and to latter-day progressives proved crucial. The efforts to preserve older forms of social relationships, to resist the rise of the "plutocracy," and to reinvigorate the ideals of democracy began at the state and local level. Popular reaction and journalistic exposure impelled policymakers toward legislative enactment and amendment and forced legal officials to initiate judicial prosecution. By the turn-of-the-century the states and people were prepared to confront corporate consolidation.

In the fall of 1889, Missouri's secretary of state, Alexander A. Lesueur, started to enforce the state's new antitrust law according to its terms. He received special support from the farmers of Missouri. The seventh annual session of the Missouri State Grange and the Bates County Farmers' and Laborers' Union both adopted resolutions that endorsed the actions of the secretary of state against corporations violating the antitrust law. They further hoped that the constitutionality and legality of the act could be established. The law provided that the secretary of state prepare a form of affidavit and send it to every corporation doing business in the state. Corporate officials would be required to sign and attest under oath that their corporation was not a party to any trust, pool, or combination, "intended to limit or fix the price or lessen the production and sale of any article of commerce, use or consumption, or to prevent . . . the manufacture or output of any such article."[1] To assist the secretary, county and city officials compiled a list of some 7,500 corporations that needed to be contacted. A few days before the deadline for returning affidavits, the *Post-Dispatch* wondered whether the antitrust law would be enforced and suggested that St. Louis would be an excellent place for a test case. Sugar, cotton oil, lead, whiskey, linseed, bagging, burial caskets, and insurance interests were all located in the city. At the same time, St. Louis Circuit Attorney Ashley C. Clover expressed his intention of asking the grand jury to investigate alleged antitrust violations in the city. When the grand jury convened for this purpose, it was the first such action since the Missouri antitrust law took effect. Thus, its members realized their need to study the new statute before any recommendations could be made. They admitted to being "at sea as to our duties,"[2] for to them, the field appeared an entirely new one.[3]

Several hundred Missouri corporations failed to return affidavits to the secretary of state's office, and a contest of the law seemed likely. According to the *Post-Dispatch*, "opposition to the trust law is strong and bitter, and neither money nor pains will be spared to defeat it when it comes into court."[4] But under the law, the duty of enforcement rested with the various prosecuting attorneys in the state. As a result, Lesueur, Clover, and Attorney General John M. Wood, met to map strategy. Lawyers for the corporations, seeking a weak point in the law, hoped to challenge the secretary of state's right to revoke corporate charters, as such power should rest with the courts alone. Late in 1889, the secretary of state sued the Simmons Hardware Company for being a member of a pool or trust. The defense argued that the antitrust law violated the U.S. and Missouri constitutions as it "cripples the obligations of contracts and interferes with the rights of corporations."[5] Additionally, the defense argued that the law forced officers of such corporations to become witnesses against themselves. The law also gave to the secretary of state power that belonged to the judiciary and attempted to deprive corporations of their charters without due process of law. After taking the matter under advisement, Judge Daniel Dillon ruled against the state on March 11, 1890.[6]

In its initial form, the Missouri antitrust law of 1889 proved a failure. But a renewed undercurrent of popular reaction, especially strong among Missouri farmers, pressed for its revival. Agrarian hostility towards privileged monopolies and inequitable tax assessments dated back many years, but not since the 1870s had farmers possessed such organized political influence. When the Missouri legislature convened in 1891, agrarian interests dominated the lower house and the farmers wasted little time in taking direct action.[7] They pushed for corporate tax reassessments on properties belonging to foreign corporations such as railroads, telegraph, bridge, loan, and trust companies. Representatives quoted figures to show that those corporations were not paying their portion of the taxation.[8] On March 20, 1891, the Senate passed the House bill, after amending it to suit the railroad and insurance lobbies by granting exemptions to those companies. The final bill required all remaining foreign corporations doing business in Missouri to incorporate under the laws of the state and pay taxes thereon.[9]

The "Binder Trust" also provoked the hostility of the Missouri Farmers' Alliance. A $35,000,000 concern based in Chicago, the American Harvester Company, was the specific culprit as it monopolized the binding twine business. Alliance action took two forms. Economically, the Alliance sought the cooperative method of retaliation by forming its own binder factory in Missouri. Politically, the Alliance applied pressure on a Missouri legislature that realized the need to exhibit some sort of anti-corporate action. In an attempt to appease the popular anger towards the binder trust and all other combines, the house initiated a new antitrust law to overcome the weaknesses in the 1889 act.[10] The Senate accepted the House bill. On April 3, 1891, Governor David R. Francis signed Missouri's second attempt to confront corporate consolidation and, hopefully, to curb corporate privileges and concentrations of economic power.[11]

Missouri's new antitrust law, however, suffered from many of the same defects and weaknesses as the first. Prosecutors did not take personal initiative and often failed to carry through on prosecutions. Corporations refused to return affidavits and enforcement agencies could not agree on jurisdiction. Secretary of State Lesueur requested annual business reports and signed affidavits from corporations stating that they were not part of any trust or pool to fix prices. When they failed to comply with the requests, Lesueur asked the prosecuting attorneys to take action. Circuit Attorney Clover brought sixty suits against such corporations in the fall of 1891 alone. Once brought into court, most corporations tardily complied with the law, paid the court costs, and had the suits dismissed. The judge let off most of the concerns with minor penalty fees. Many delinquents were smaller companies. The major businesses of assumed trust connections regularly returned their signed affidavits. The law had no force unless a prosecutor had proof or voluntarily searched for it.[12]

Circumstances also hindered the easy enforcement of the Missouri antitrust law in 1891. Popular indignation, which had been building against industrial combinations or trusts since the late 1880s, had not yet been directed against a specific trust or an acute economic grievance. Additionally, severe economic distress had failed to affect a broad cross section of American society and provide the potential for uniting people with common grievances. The investigative reporting of a pre-muckraking newspaper had not yet expressed itself, and thus sharpened civic consciousness, magnified the economic complaints of individuals, and assisted in providing the proof needed by prosecuting attorneys. A Missouri corporation had yet to expose itself so that, within the limited early antitrust laws, legal demands might most easily be made for information and testimony. Furthermore, an energetic prosecutor had not yet appeared to lead an investigation.

The depression, which struck the nation in 1893, provided the significant catalyst for uniting people behind the antitrust issue. It heightened their sense of civic consciousness. Industrialization and urbanization, which had been growing at such a phenomenal rate, suddenly brought sever unemployment, burdensome taxes, and consumer pressures. In cities like St. Louis in the late 1880s, people had begun to question violations of their unwritten "civic contract" that promised goods at fair prices and services at efficient operation. They also questioned the role of monopoly in disrupting this contract. These changes prompted Missourians to examine the process of economic growth itself and, as consumers and taxpayers, to forcefully complain about the effects of economic consolidation.

In 1893 and 1894 the Kansas City fire insurance rating board, known as the Kansas City Board of Fire Underwriters, made drastic rate increases to its policyholders. Most of the increases ranged from 20 to 80 percent, but in some instances rate increases soared from 100 to 300 percent. The head of the Kansas City board, William J. Fetter, became known widely as the "rate Czar." He, like most fire insurance company heads, favored rate increases as a means of keeping the companies solvent during the depression.[13] They also sought to pad their margin of risk should certain privately owned, fire-fighting water companies go bankrupt. When James R. Waddill, state superintendent of insurance, issued his annual report in 1893, he agreed that fire losses in Missouri had increased, and that many fire insurance companies had lost money. A number of companies actually had withdrawn from the state. Those that remained became more cautious and "considerably advanced the rates of insurance." But the superintendent admitted the existence of "very decided protests, and much dissatisfaction expressed in many quarters at this advance of fire insurance rates."[14] One year later, when Waddill again made his report, he referred to his previous evaluation which had justified rate increases, but his opinion had changed somewhat. In 1894 he was "inclined to believe also that in some instances the underwriters took advantage of a necessity for a reasonable increase of rates and raised them unreasonably, and made them quite burdensome to policy-holders." The superintendent found that rates had been raised on communities and districts where no loss by fire had occurred for years and where the companies had done a profitable business. In his opinion the companies had prejudiced themselves in the judgment of the people.[15]

People had already stopped listening to explanations and had begun to talk of an insurance combine. According to the *Jefferson City Tribune*, a general uproar existed all over the state against exorbitant fire insurance rates, and many people believed that there must be just cause for so much complaint. There seemed to be no justice in allowing fire insurance companies to form pools, destroy competition, and impose unjust rates upon the public. The editors of the *Mexico Intelligencer* called the advance in existing rates, "robbery." Rates in Mexico, Missouri, had jumped from 20 to 80 percent even though the town's taxpayers had spent thousands of dollars building new water works. Many people believed that instead of increased fire insurance rates, there should be a substantial reduction. According to the people of Mexico, the insurance companies benefited chiefly from a water system that cost taxpayers $2,500 a year. The editors of the *Intelligencer* realized that the increase in rates would be severe on town property owners, as current rates were already "exceedingly burdensome." The editors suggested, as an effective remedy against such an economic injustice, the organization of a local fire insurance company. Aware of the larger problem, one reader complained that the increased rates were not only burdensome, but out of proportion to the profits of legitimate business. "In all the ordinary lines of business sharp competition has naturally reduced the profits of trade to a close margin. The insurance companies, however, by combination manage to increase their charges." [16] One fire insurance agent in Independence agreed with these consumer-taxpayer complaints. Although he felt that rates in his city needed revisions, he characterized the new rates as being "entirely out of proportion." [17]

The Kansas City Board of Fire Underwriters also could be guilty of corporate arrogance. After raising fire insurance rates nearly 100 percent in some instances, Fetter proposed to reduce rates 10 percent if the city of Mexico would eliminate its insurance license fee. The townspeople adamantly opposed it: "They should pay license [tax] the same as any other business enterprise. . . . If they do not want to do business here let them get out." [18] Consumer-taxpayer problems with the insurance "combine," just like farmers' problems with the Harvester Trust two years before, revealed for Missourians the effects of economic consolidation on their everyday lives.

The Missouri antitrust law remained an ineffective instrument during the early debate over fire insurance rates. One major weakness occurred because the divided duties of the attorney general and the secretary of state effectively shielded trust organizations from prosecution. The secretary of state accepted affidavits without investigation by the attorney general's office. Attorney General Robert F. Walker stood firm in his statements that such responsibility rested with Secretary of State Lesueur. Interviews granted the *Post-Dispatch* by various state attorneys general indicated that the low pay of those officials and the possibilities of accepting fees from private corporations provided the potential for conflicts of interest. This may well have contributed to the lack of vigorous antitrust enforcement. Appointments, made by such officials, also could favor corporate interests. Evidence materialized that strongly suggested that district attorneys freely engaged in private practice.[19] When Lesueur began his annual affidavit process, the *Post-Dispatch* balked, explaining it "a matter of notoriety that there are corporations in this State which violate the law and are in trusts and combines."[20] According to the editors of the *Post-Dispatch*, the attorney general would have to be made responsible for enforcement.[21]

When forty-three St. Louis corporations again failed to return their antitrust affidavits, the anger of St. Louis' major newspaper intensified. "Is it any wonder that anarchy thrives when rich and powerful combines violate the laws and defy State authority with impunity, and when they rob and oppress the people despite restraining laws?"[22] In October, 1894, the *Post-Dispatch* ran a full, front-page cartoon entitled "They'll Neither Fish Nor Cut Bait—The Reason Why Missouri's Anti-Trust Law is Not Enforced." The cartoon portrayed Missouri Attorney General Walker, Secretary of State Lesueur, and Circuit Attorney William Zachritz lounging under a shade tree and smoking Missouri corncobs as their fishing poles (labeled "the law," "the people," and "the press") dangled unattended. Various trust serpents still waited beneath the surface to be caught. The editorial comment accompanying the cartoon accused the officials of being blind to the "reptile" trusts swarming in Missouri's "business pool . . . eating up all the little fish," and "fattening up on illegal profits." While these activities remained visible to everyone else, Missouri's legal officials had not hooked a single trust.[23]

The editors of the *Post-Dispatch* complained that proceedings, when begun at all, involved only small companies, and had not touched the major St. Louis concerns known to belong to the great trusts. As a cynical example they cited the Beckley Café Company "which might possibly enter into a combine to regulate the price of quail on toast." Trusts, said to exist in the city, included the Electric Light Trust, Sugar Trust, Cordage Trust, Linseed Oil Trust, Lead Trust, Rubber Trust, Whiskey Trust, Kerosene Oil and Petroleum Trust, and the Cotton Oil Trust. According to the *Post-Dispatch*, the "matter is one which is causing no end of comment by the public at large."[24] Even businessmen became outspoken in their self-assurance. One remarked: "The truth of the business is that the laws against the trusts are like a sieve and will not hold. I have . . . closely watched the legislation against trusts, but I have yet to see anyone convicted under the laws enacted against them."[25]

In response to the complaints of major dailies like the *Post-Dispatch*, and undoubtedly to the embarrassment of its own failure to structure a solid antitrust statute, the Missouri legislature passed its third antitrust law. Both political parties had introduced antitrust proposals as popular appeals to the entire state and to "an active popular demand."[26] The new law improved the earlier statute by authorizing the attorney general to bring suit against companies that neglected to report to the secretary of state. But the influence of lobbying tactics in Jefferson City fundamentally crippled the legislation. Just as the railroad lobby dominated consideration of anti-corporate measures in prior legislative sessions, the insurance lobby showed how easy representative government could be thwarted in 1895.[27]

Rural representatives strongly supported the original provisions that would have placed all insurance companies, doing business through boards of underwriters, under the antitrust law. Conscious of a hostile public, they asserted boldly on the floor of the assembly that "their people had been robbed until they had arisen in indignant protest."[28] Two hundred petitioners from Warrensburg and Johnson County emphasized this point as they sent a memorial to the Missouri legislature in agreement with the original antitrust provisions. As policy-holders, they referred to the recent "arbitrary" advance in rates and demanded "protection from the importunate greed of foreign insurance companies doing business in this State and which have combined as a trust under the name of the Association of Fire Underwriters of Missouri."[29] Such sentiments were not uncommon. When an agent for the Citizens' Fire Association of Mankato, Minnesota, arrived in Sedalia, Missouri, to see about organizing a mutual insurance company, the editors of the *Weekly Gazette* commented that his arrival promised "relief to property owners from the extortion of insurance companies. The highway robbery methods of the companies in raising the price of insurance is too well-known to need explanation.[30]

The efforts of Missourians to secure a conclusive antitrust law proved unsuccessful. A powerful lobby, which included a union of two groups, ably controlled the final formation of the bill. James A. Waterworth, head of the St. Louis Board of Fire Underwriters, led the insurance interests from that city, supported by his board's legislative committee and some sixty prominent St. Louis businessmen.[31] William J. Fetter supplied the leadership for the Kansas City board and Kansas City businessmen. Their efforts resulted in the exemption from the bill of the insurance interests based in Kansas City and St. Louis—as "cities of over 100,000 inhabitants." The remainder of the state fell under the new law. Since firms based in the two major cities wrote 75 percent of the insurance business, the new law could not quite be called a triumph for popular government.[32]

Other states experienced difficulties similar to those Missouri encountered with antitrust enforcement. In March, 1893, a Minnesota legislative committee undertook an investigation of the alleged coal combine in that state. In Minnesota, instead of leaving the courts to "palter with the law" and favor the combine, "as has been the case in most States where the question has arisen," the legislature took direct action.[33] It asserted its right to inspect the books of corporations and to present its evidence to the grand jury. The committee filed its report and charged that a coal combine, known as the Minnesota Bureau of Coal Statistics, existed in the state. The report concluded that the Bureau had been able to force non-subscribers out of busi-

ness, and had greatly raised the price of anthracite coal to consumers in Minnesota and Wisconsin. The committee, aided by
the Minnesota attorney general, prepared cases against the
central figures of the combine, but the grand jury failed to return any indictments. However, strong popular feelings against
the alleged coal trust prompted Governor Knute Nelson of
Minnesota to call for an antitrust convention to discuss the
problems caused by monopoly. Twenty-five governors responded and promised to send delegates. The convention actually took place in Chicago during the first week in June, 1893,
but achieved no major results.[34]

Even though state antitrust victories were slow in coming,
persistent efforts underscored the larger questions of democracy and economic freedom involved in the struggle. In Illinois,
Attorney General M. J. Maloney boldly confronted the problem
of uncontrolled economic consolidation. During his first sixteen
months in office, Maloney instituted common law suits against
the Whiskey Trust (the corporate title of which was the Distillers' and Cattle Feeders' Company), the School Furniture Trust,
the Chicago Gas Trust, and the Tobacco Trust.[35] In an interview granted to the *Post-Dispatch* in May of 1894, Maloney also
stated that he intended to institute antitrust proceedings against
the Chicago packing houses, the Chicago grain elevators, and
against some 3,000 to 4,000 business concerns that had failed
to comply with the request of the secretary of state and furnish
an affidavit that they did not belong to any trust. Unlike the
procedure prevalent in Missouri, the Illinois attorney general
intended to challenge the most offensive companies, those
known to belong to trusts openly and flagrantly in violation of
the law. To Maloney, the immense wealth of the trusts was their
only strength, and the enforcement of the state antitrust laws
was necessitated by this "condition of the country." Maloney
recalled statistics showing that 47 percent of the population
controlled the majority of wealth in the country in 1861, while
in 1894 control was in the hands of 12 percent. "If this does not
show monopoly and the centralizing effect of monopoly I am
very much mistaken. . . . We may talk of democracy and equal
rights all we please, but this country is to-day in danger from
an evil . . . the evil of raising up a privileged class to prosper

and grow rich at the unfair expense of the masses."[36] Trusts were intolerable and the Illinois attorney general, by word and by example, provided motivation and direction towards confronting that problem.

Missourians easily noted the discrepancy between the energetic example of antitrust enforcement being set by Maloney in Illinois and the apathetic response of Missouri's own legal officials in the events that surrounded the bridge monopoly in St. Louis in 1895. In February of that year, St. Louisans heard allegations that a corporation, known as the Terminal Railroad Association, controlled the two existing bridges (Eads Bridge and Merchants Bridge) linking their city with Illinois and the East. In spite of strong evidence to support the accusations of the St. Louis press, Missouri legislators and legal officials failed to take immediate action. As in earlier instances, the frustrations of the public with their elected representatives, and the embarrassment of those state officials, were heightened when the Illinois legislature ordered its own investigation of the "bridge bandits."[37]

After a thorough study, the Illinois Senate Bridge Investigating Committee submitted its report. The report acknowledged evidence of a pooling agreement and triggered federal involvement. As the bridge combine affected the flow of interstate commerce, any improprieties would be in violation of federal statutes and under federal jurisdiction. As a result, the federal government ordered a grand jury investigation. The composition of the grand jury included a large majority of men who "were representatives of corporate interests and whose aggregate wealth is established in the neighborhood of $15,000,000."[38] The *Post-Dispatch* found this predominance of wealth to be disconcerting. When the grand jury came within one vote of the three-fourths needed to recommend against the alleged combine, the *Post-Dispatch* leveled charges of bribery and bias.[39] Illinois State Senator James R. Campbell, chairman of the Illinois investigating committee, agreed:

I don't see how such a thing could be done and it certainly looks bad for the Federal Grand Jury. Why we brought out enough testimony to convict the whole crowd and turned over . . . signed documents that are in themselves prima facie evidence of the existence of a pool. They show not only a tonnage combine but a money pool as well. One of these documents shows the percentage each company receives of the joint earnings and if one carried more than another it was obligated to pay it to the company falling below the agreed percentage.[40]

A member of the St. Louis Manufacturers' Association appeared equally exasperated: "Such proceedings make a travesty of justice. If it had been some poor fellow charged with cutting timber on government land he would have been in jail long ago."[41] The power of consolidated capital, the apparent apathy of their own state officers, and what appeared as federal acquiescence to the process of monopolization, served as reminders of injustice to Missourians who struggled to weather the severe economic depression. The fate of the antitrust movement may not have stirred much anxiety in corporate board rooms, but the totality of the failure served as an ominous comment on the condition of popular democracy.

By the mid–1890s, explanations for the failure of national and state antitrust statutes measured the sophistication of the society. Many people believed that the primary reason lay in defective legislation. Others found inadequate enforcement to be a more basic explanation. The *Post-Dispatch* undoubtedly echoed the sentiments of many. In January, 1897, the newspaper editorialized that the people sought an antitrust law that the trusts must obey.[42] The objective seemed to be a successfully proven (statute enforced) model law, such as those in Texas and Georgia, that all states might copy.[43] Between 1890 and 1900 this quest for more enforceable legal instruments increased the number of states and territories which prohibited trusts by law from thirteen to twenty-seven. In addition, many states, like Missouri, continued to pass legislative revisions to their original statutes.[44]

Not everyone, however, was preoccupied with this "more law" solution. The *Kansas City Times* acknowledged the popular trend but focused on a different reason for the failure to produce antitrust convictions. According to the *Times*, the "movement" to improve the law was "largely in response to public sentiment . . . and intensified by the continued exactions of

conscienceless combines of capital, operating to crush out competition and extort exorbitant prices from consumers."[45] The
paper further noted that considerable impetus and encourage-
ment had come from states that had passed "effective" antitrust laws. But the *Times* quickly stressed its opinion that Missouri already had an excellent law which, "if vigorously
enforced," would do away with all trusts operating in the state.[46]
The success of Missouri's antitrust law from this point forward
is really the story of consolidating corporate power, popular reaction heightened by persistent journalistic exposure, and cru-
sading reform from the Missouri attorney general's office that
continued throughout the Progressive Era.

On July 23, 1897, the *Kansas City Times* offered an excellent
example of the country's centralized wealth in the hands of a
few, and related how Missourians were forced to contribute. The
Times reported that in 1896 Kansas Citians paid nearly $800,000
in fire insurance premiums. However, fire losses totaled only
about $200,000. In the opinion of the *Times*, these figures indi-
cated that at least $400,000 had been stolen from Kansas City
through exorbitant fire insurance rates. Allegedly, Kansas City
property owners paid rates almost double those charged in most
of Missouri outside the two major cities where the "combine"
still operated. In St. Louis the situation was reported as being
several times more severe.[47]

Figures illustrated that the profits of the large insurance concerns with a capital stock of at least $1,000,000, in many cases,
had ranged from $250,000 to $300,000 in one year. Readers easily saw that these robust profits had been made during what,
to most of them, had been depression years. How could the
great depression of the 1890s allow the insurance business to
amass the largest profits in its history? Missourians formulated
their conclusion. An insurance trust had extorted money from
policyholders. While the people suffered, the insurance combine had piled up its profits. Prosperity had been stolen. The
raw facts supported the popular conclusion.[48]

Rising insurance rates contributed just one of the problems
facing workers, consumers, and taxpayers in Missouri during
the depression years of the 1890s. Unemployment, rampant tax
inequities, and faltering civic services all stirred a rising civic

discontent. In St. Louis, such organizations as the Single Tax League focused public complaints on taxes. At the same time, the St. Louis Socialist Labor Party emphasized public works for unemployment relief and tax reform to aid small property owners. The year 1895 witnessed the formation of the St. Louis Civic Federation. During its first two years in existence, the organization brought together conservative mugwumps, middle-class reformers, and some reform-minded labor leaders from the Central Trades and Labor Union. These segments of St. Louis society joined the list of those concerned about municipal services and tax reform. All three groups coalesced around the issue of tax reform and the problem of public utility assessment.

Public hostility to the perennial, underhanded manner in which municipal franchises had been given away forced the Missouri legislature to take action, and revived the popularity of the tax-reform issue. In 1895, legislators passed a law that required all streetcar, gas, water, and electric franchises to be sold in open bid. In St. Louis, ex-state labor commissioner Lee Meriwether became the most outspoken political champion of tax reform. As labor commissioner, Meriwether had made a thorough study of street railways in Kansas City and St. Louis. He discovered a drastic underassessment of all municipal street railways. While the assessment for urban property owners averaged a rate of 40 percent, street railway assessment only ranged from 11 to 25 percent. According to Meriwether, while some tax collectors had "possessed the eyes of a lynx in detecting the sewing machine of a poor seamstress or the tools of a mechanic and selling them for taxes, the same officials have been too blind to see miles of track and hundreds of cars subject under the laws to taxation."[49] As an unsuccessful tax-reform candidate for mayor of St. Louis in 1897, Meriwether polled 20,000 votes in the Democratic primary. The popularity of the tax reform issue during the depression gave a good indication of the distress felt by many citizens. The depression had hurt people economically, it had increased their civic consciousness, and, in the process, it had intensified their anger. The crusade for insurance reform both incorporated and augmented this emerging consumer-taxpayer reaction. Missouri's newly elected Attorney General Edward C. Crow smartly sensed the popular mood, and, being reform-minded like Meriwether, he sought to lead it.[50]

The exposures of the *Kansas City Times* aroused the attention of Missouri's attorney general. In announcing his intention to investigate the alleged fire insurance trust on August 7, 1897, Crow stated that he would take action, in part, because of complaints of excessive fire insurance rates that had come to him from Kansas City. However, he went on to note that the problem was statewide. "Every man who has to carry insurance in Missouri is a victim of this trust."[51] Complaints, in fact, had come from all over Missouri, and many country newspapers vociferously condemned the trust. The *Times* listed sixteen rural newspapers that had written letters to the *Times* in support of the antitrust crusade initiated by that newspaper.[52] The editorial comments from the *Mexico Intelligencer* appeared typical of most of the remarks: "For years the insurance combine has ridden rough shod over the property owners of Missouri. . . . They have made arbitrary rates, in utter disregard of fairness, and have snapped their fingers in the face of the public whenever protest has been made."[53] In response to this popular pressure, Attorney General Crow, on September 6, filed suits against a long list of insurance companies. He accused them of combining to regulate and fix rates on premiums to be paid for insuring property in violation of the antitrust law. The suits, in effect, embodied two separate contests. In the first suit, Crow sought to challenge the constitutionality of the 1895 and 1897 Missouri antitrust statutes that exempted insurance companies in the state's two major cities. In the second suit the attorney general hoped to find the Kansas City Board of Fire Underwriters (the Fetter Bureau) guilty of operating to regulate rates outside of that city.[54]

Crow's first suit (against the Aetna and twenty-two other foreign insurance companies) formally began in March of 1898. The attorney general charged the twenty-three companies with being members of a trust known as the Western Insurance Union. Sam Davis, appointed by the Missouri Supreme Court to be special commissioner, Attorney General Crow and Superintendent of Insurance Edward T. Orear formed the court of inquiry and took testimony from mebers of the Union during the spring and summer of that year. Crow's hopes for a quick victory ended, however, on December 14, when the Supreme Court of Missouri denied his writ of ouster and upheld the constitutionality of the law. However, victory arose from this defeat. Popular support for Crow's actions and the negative response of the court prompted a vigorous campaign for antitrust revision of the insurance exemption in the 1899 session of the general assembly. Governor Lon V. Stephens gave the insurance issue special treatment during his first biennial message to the Missouri legislature on January 5, 1899. In his speech Stephens called attention to a provision that had been inserted in the amended Missouri antitrust law of 1895 which exempted insurance companies in cities of 100,000 inhabitants. The governor looked upon such a provision as an admission that an insurance trust existed in Kansas City and St. Louis. He recommended its repeal. The insurance lobby still had a few friends in the House and Senate, "but several able and rising Senators now pressed the [amended antitrust] bill. Senators Morton, Major, McClintic, Farris, Dowell . . . all inflamed with the current anti-monopolistic sentiment . . . swept everything before them."[55] During the first week in April the Farris antitrust bill emerged from the assembly with the St. Louis and Kansas City boards of underwriters incorporated into the general antitrust law. On April 18, 1899, Governor Stephens signed the Farris bill, forcing the St. Louis and Kansas City boards to disband.[56]

The second investigation undertaken by Crow proved far more intriguing. It showed that vigorous enforcement, activated by popular pressure, could make the antitrust law a viable instrument against corporate collusion. The attorney general hoped to show that an organization, known as the St. Joseph Social Club, existed for the non-social purpose of fixing insurance rates. If this allegation could be proven in a city the size of St. Joseph (less than 100,000 inhabitants and not under the antitrust exemption), the insurance companies involved could be ousted from doing business in the state. Crow and Superintendent of Insurance Orear, supported by the testimony of insurance agent James J. Garth of St. Joseph, felt they had an excellent opportunity to make a case. They set out to collect further evidence.[57]

The inquiry began in St. Joseph on March 11, 1898, and immediately produced results. Testimony revealed that the "social club" consisted only of insurance agents. Daily reports, according to statements made by agent Fred A. H. Garlichs, were submitted to the secretary of the club, showing the business done by all agents (members). The secretary examined the reports to see if they had been written according to the Fetter rate book, the schedule used by the Kansas City Board of Fire Underwriters. Garlichs denied, however, that a combine existed. He claimed that the club served merely to simplify the adjustment of claims made by various companies that had secured risks on the same plant or building. Garth, however, challenged the testimony of Garlichs and stated that the members of the club signed an agreement that bound them not to make any rates below those in the rate book. But as damaging as Garth's testimony was, the real blow to the insurance trust came from William J. Fetter, the "rate Czar." Under questioning, Fetter admitted that the Kansas City Board of Fire Underwriters maintained rates, and that rate reports were sent to him to be checked for conformity. Only he had the authority to raise or lower fire and tornado insurance rates in Kansas City (or in any city using his rate book). As Fetter arrogantly put it, his rates were "not reviewable by any power on earth."[58] If an agent violated the rules of the board of underwriters, he faced a fine and penalty.[59]

By the time Crow was ready to argue and submit his case to the Missouri Supreme Court, on April 29, 1899, the complete details of the St. Joseph-Kansas City rate combine had been brought out. The suit itself charged the Firemen's Fund and seventy-two other insurance companies with combining to fix rates in violation of the antitrust law. The seventy-three companies held memberships in the St. Joseph Social Club, a rate-conforming organization, bound by rules, and operating under the guise of a social brotherhood. Crow convincingly had shown that the companies employed Fetter to make rate estimates for all of Missouri outside of Kansas City and St. Louis. The companies paid him nine-tenths of one percent of the premiums on all business, a salary of from $30,000 to $40,000 a year. Fetter carefully did not deal directly with the agents. He induced the St. Joseph club to employ as secretary E. F. Scott, from Fetter's

Kansas City office. Scott made the rates on new risks and suggested changes, but always mailed these to Fetter. Fetter then
mailed them to the companies, and the companies sent them
to their agents. If agents did not write policies at the Fetter rate,
Scott returned the policies to the agents for revision. The agent
then paid a $50 fine for the first offense and lost his agency for
the second. The companies paid the salary of the secretary and
the expenses of the club, which showed that they had knowledge of the arrangements and actions being conducted.[60]

On June 30, 1899, the Missouri Supreme Court awarded a writ
of ouster against the seventy-three foreign insurance companies doing business in St. Joseph. The court found the underwriters' social club of St. Joseph to be "a plain, palpable, but
bungling pool, trust, agreement, combination, confederation and
understanding organized to evade the antitrust laws of Missouri."[61] This was the first instance of the state's enforcement
of the law since the initial legislative enactment ten years before. Two weeks later the state supreme court modified its order of ouster and allowed the companies to remain in Missouri
if they each paid a $1,000 fine to the state school fund and the
costs of litigation. Since the initiation of the suit, fire insurance
rates in Missouri dropped 25 percent on all retail lumber yards,
dwellings, private barns, churches, schoolhouses, courthouses,
and jails; 15 to 25 percent on brick store buildings; 50 percent
on tornado and cyclone policies; and 25 percent on all farm
risks.[62]

The convictions, fines, and rate reductions proved important
to citizens, taxpayers, and consumers. However, the deeper
significance of the case lay in the process that brought about
success. As consumers, Missourians had complained of unjust
insurance rates as early as 1895. The *Kansas City Times* took the
complaints seriously and began their own investigation. The
exposés of the *Times* not only provided details of the rate grievances, but also confirmed popular suspicions that insurance
corporations had used economic hard times to expand their
margins of profit. As a rationale in defense of the rate increases, the trust claimed inadequate water pressure or fire
prevention agencies. When municipalities made these improvements, however, the people found only slight relief as in-

surance consumers. At the same time, they faced increased hardship as taxpayers. The revelations of the *Times* and the complaints of Missouri's rural press, prompted Attorney General Crow and Insurance Superintendent Orear to take action. Officials of the attorney general's office traveled over 6,000 miles across the nation, taking testimony from the home offices of the various insurance companies.[63] This merging of grievance, heightened awareness, and enforcement had proven successful and had established a model for the state antitrust movement and for progressivism.

In the spring and summer of 1899, the focus of antitrust activity shifted from a local-state to a regional-national orientation. Prompted by recent events and a desire to devise new ways and means of solidifying the forces of opposition to monopoly, Governor Joseph D. Sayers of Texas issued a call for an antitrust convention of governors and attorneys general of the Southern and Western states. The Texas governor, in cooperation with Governor Stephens of Missouri, scheduled the convention to convene in St. Louis on September 20, 1899. As a further indication of the general interest in the question of trusts and the desire for open discussion on the subject, the Civic Federation of Chicago issued its own call for a national conference on trusts. The Chicago conference was to meet a week before the St. Louis convention, and the list of participants included governors, attorneys general, lawyers, scholars, and representatives of labor, agriculture, and commerce.[64]

Rather than remain content with the state antitrust laws, Attorney General Crow and other state officials looked toward a solution that would prevent the formation of trusts in the first place. Crow knew from the insurance investigation that trusts could be restrained and dissolved by the legal process of the state courts. He also realized that it was much easier to create a trust than it was to destroy one. To demolish a trust often required years of expensive and exhaustive trial process by the state. The calls for the regional and national conventions provided opportunities to move toward the goals of prevention. The Chicago conference merely provided a forum for theoretical debate. However, the St. Louis convention passed a set of practical resolutions which recommended new federal and state

statutes for the suppression of trusts. Most of the resolutions
involved changes in corporation laws such as increasing the li-
ability of shareholders, limiting corporations in their operations
between the different states, and placing foreign corporations
on an equal basis with domestic corporations.[65]

The critical gap in the debate over legal provisions was a lack
of direct concern for the effects of monopoly on the lives of
people. In a brief speech presenting the resolutions to the St.
Louis convention, Governor Benton McMillan of Tennessee
(chairman of the resolutions committee) confronted the fundamental implications of trust formation. McMillan acknowledged that the nation's resources had been developed by the
exertions of both individuals and corporations. However, the
point had been reached where corporations sought to combine
to reap benefits for a few at the expense of everyone else. To
the governor, the logical conclusion of the trust system was self-
evident—one universal trust, controlled by a few individuals,
would dictate the price of labor, the price of raw materials, and
the price of the manufactured products.[66]

Trusts not only controlled the economic process, but human
relationships as well. Governor Hazen Pingree of Michigan explored this dilemma at the Chicago conference. In gathering
material for use at the conference, the Civic Federation of Chicago sent out circulars containing some sixty-nine questions. Of
the sixty-nine, Pingree found only one that in any way related
to the effects of trusts upon society: "In all the discussion of
trusts, there is no indication that any thought whatever has been
given to their effect upon our national life, upon our citizenship, and upon the lives and characters of the men and women
who are the real strength of our republic." The trust made it
impossible for the individual businessman to continue to operate on a small, independent scale. As the trust concentrated
the ownership and management of business in fewer hands, it
forced the individual businessman to concede and become a trust
employee. "Self-preservation compels it. Duty to his family forces
him to it." Foremen and workers had no choice but to follow
their old employer and surrender their traditional, close association between worker and employer. They became recruits in
a "vast industrial army with no hopes and no aspirations—a

daily task to perform and no personal interest and perhaps no pride in the success of their work." Their self-identity disappeared. They became "cogs and little wheels in a great complicated machine." In the almost "insane desire" to control trade, ambition and perhaps even inventive genius were "deadened and killed." As the degrading process of trust consolidation destroyed equality of economic opportunity, it threatened the democratic principles premised upon that opportunity.[67]

By the turn-of-the-century more and more people felt the injustices inflicted by the combinations of capital, and better understood the workings of the trust process. This was revealed by numerous accounts that appeared in Missouri newspapers. The *Lexington Intelligencer* told of a certain farmer who, in March of 1897, brought twelve hogs to Centralia, Missouri, and sold them for a sum of $104.10. With this sum the farmer went shopping. At the hardware store he bought three kegs of nails at $1.78 each, 200 pounds of wire at $1.90 per hundred, a cook stove for $30, 100 feet of screening at 85 cents, a plow for $10, and other small items which cost $11.62. He then went to the drug store and purchased $10.50 worth of patent medicines and drugs, and finished his day of shopping by purchasing 180 pounds of sugar for $10. This left him something over $20 to pay for his doctor bill and newspaper subscription. Two years later this farmer did some comparison shopping. This time he sold thirteen hogs for which he received the same price per pound for a total of $105. He then spent $3.50 for each keg of nails and $3.10 per hundred pounds of wire. The same stove cost $38, the screen $1.50, the plow $12.50, the same bill of small hardware items $16.40, drugs $17, and 180 pounds of sugar $11.25. Adding up his bill the farmer found himself in debt $8.33, with nothing left to pay the doctor or newspaper.[68]

The consumer awareness of the Centralia farmer, much like that of the earlier insurance subscribers, merely confirmed the obvious. Forced to pay more for goods, protection, or service, they received no comparable "break" as producers, consumers, or taxpayers. The farmer paid more for every item on his shopping list, but witnessed no improvement in the price paid to him for his hogs. Property owners paid increased fire insurance rates even with excellent fire prevention records. They also failed to receive any reduction in rates when, as taxpayers, they paid for improved water works in their cities. As they searched for an explanation, they found an artificially controlled economic system. The trusts controlled the market price for hogs and imposed prices on the cost of insurance, plows, sugar, nails, and wire. Virtual trust control over production and consumption, markets and services placed producers and consumers in a situation of economic dependence.

MODERNIZATION AND THE ANTI-MONOPOLY ISSUE: THE ST. LOUIS STREETCAR STRIKE OF 1900

The cooperation that had been shown by producers, small retailers, and consumers since the late 1880s in resisting trust control over production, consumption, markets, and services continued throughout the 1890s and into the early years of the new century. Capitalists continued to amass great fortunes and create vast corporate empires, and by the year 1900 the pace of consolidation had quickened so that nearly 300 trusts existed. People had ample opportunity to learn about these momentous economic changes through newspaper accounts and campaign speeches, but they also felt the influences of those industrial developments on their everyday lives. They came into contact with the process of corporate modernization in the use of daily goods and services. The St. Louis transit strike of 1900 provides an excellent example of the way in which the people of one city reacted to that process, and the ways in which workers and streetcar consumers cooperated to meet the challenge.

The transit strike in St. Louis focused the issue of monopolization for many residents of the city. Moving from feelings of anger toward the streetcar companies, the strike forced citizens of St. Louis to come to grips with issues broader than the immediate confrontation between workers and employers. As the strike dragged on, the people saw the results of monopolistic consolidation granted the streetcar companies by the legislature. As citizens, taxpayers, and voters they objected to the legislature's failure to keep antitrust promises and establish a law for the taxation of franchises. The company's refusal to ac-

cept arbitration reinforced their perceptions of antisocial corporate behavior. In addition, the appearance of outsiders as
strikebreakers and reminders that foreign capitalists controlled
the transportation system of St. Louis threatened the community values which brought St. Louisans of many different classes
together. The extension of the strike to include posse and police protection of the corporation, plus executive indifference to
popular opinion, exposed the issue of corporate privilege which
trampled the rights of citizens, homeowners, and taxpayers.

The depression of the 1890s focused public attention on the
conduct of municipal services, as information circulated that
certain businesses had avoided paying their full tax assessments. In 1895 Lee Meriwether, State Labor Commissioner,
gained recognition as an advocate of the taxation of municipal
franchises and the reassessment of property taxes. Newspapers
such as the *St. Louis Post-Dispatch* intensified the tax issue by
charging that street railway companies in that city obtained tax
breaks through pressure applied to the Board of Assessors and
the Board of Equalization. Public antagonism toward the streetcar companies increased with reports of accidents caused by
fenderless cars with bad brakes, increased fares, and damages
caused by uncontrolled street construction. In the mayoral
campaign of 1897, Lee Meriwether made a strong, independent
challenge to the regular party candidates, running on the issue
of taxation and regulation of public service corporations. Meriwether's efforts merged with those of the Single Tax League in
the late 1890s and forced Mayor Henry Ziegenhein to persuade
the Board of Assessors to increase the assessments on the tan-
gible property of street railways in 1899. But even with the consolidation of most of the street railway network in St. Louis,
service deteriorated. The distance between stops lengthened and
the number of cars decreased, but the number of passengers
continued to increase.[1]

St. Louisans frequently complained of the poor quality of
service and the attitude of corporate arrogance manifested by
the traction companies. It seemed to many that a quasi-public
corporation should exhibit a semblance of courtesy and efficiency in exchange for the franchise privileges granted by the
city. In January, 1898, Mr. F. DeDonato, a citizen of St. Louis,

was brought into court and fined $10 for threatening a streetcar motorman with a gun. Mr. DeDonato and several members of his family were going home on a Suburban Street Railway Company car and disembarked at Hamilton and Plymouth Avenues. The roads were muddy and the family was picking its way across the street when another streetcar approached. Thinking the motorman had no intention of stopping the car, Mr. DeDonato pulled a revolver. His action resulted in the fine. On appeal, the decision was reversed and Judge David Murphy took the opportunity to express his opinion regarding corporations in general. The Judge stated: "Even if Mr. DeDonato pulled a gun he had a right to do so. Citizens have rights that corporations must respect. If Mr. DeDonato thought his life or his family in danger he had a right to protect them. The street railways don't own this court."[2] If a general attitude of disaffection had not yet turned to open disenchantment, the state's elected policymakers seemed bent upon hastening the transition.

On May 17, 1899, the *Post-Dispatch* accused the state legislature of being "packed with paid agents of the street railway syndicate." The legislature was about to vote on a railway consolidation bill which the newspaper regarded as a betrayal of the public interest. The bill would "create the worse kind of monopoly—a monopoly of franchise privileges." The measure granted authority to any municipal street railway corporation to acquire, by lease or purchase, the property of any other street railroad. Two days later the newspaper's worst fears were realized when, by a vote of 91 to 38, with all St. Louis members but one in support, the House joined with the Senate "in turning over the cities of the state to a monster street railway combine."[3] Attorney General Edward C. Crow concurred and warned the legislators that the bill was plainly a trust proposition and detrimental to the interests of consumers: "If this bill passes the people of St. Louis will have no protection in the matter of service that the monopoly will furnish. The monopoly will do as it pleases."[4]

Governor Lon V. Stephens exercised his prerogative and signed the "Street Railway Bill," but the negative reaction to the measure was so severe that it forced him to defend his action. Governor Stephens failed to see the threat of monopoly and supported the bill on three points: consolidation would enable workingmen to obtain transfers; price increases would be impossible (for reasons not stated); and a rival street railroad might be authorized at any time as a competitor. When asked whether consolidation would lead to undue political power through the combine's control over several thousand employees, Stephens responded in the negative: "What difference would there be in this behalf, whether one man, acting through separate corporate organizations, managed or controlled four or five roads, or that the same man should do the same thing under one corporate organization?"[5] The rationale behind this statement dumbfounded the editors of the *Post-Dispatch* who rhetorically asked: "Why not apply this argument to the Standard Oil Trust, the Sugar Trust, the Steel Trust, the Tobacco Trust, and the hundred trusts that are now menacing the industrial and political freedom of the American people? Is this a valid argument in favor of trusts or is it a pitiable excuse for subservience to a trust?"[6]

Regarding the new law as an invitation to consolidation, the United Railways Company,[7] a corporation chartered by the state of Missouri, proposed in late July to acquire the railroad lines, properties, and franchises of all the independent railroad systems in St. Louis except the Suburban. The consolidation scheme was so structured as to include a reserve clause in which $4 million in bonds would be set aside for the acquisition of the Suburban system at a future date. Company officials promised the public more efficient service and better facilities when the modernized streetcar system became an accomplished fact. The *Post-Dispatch* could do no more than lament the consolidation, which became final on September 30, 1899, operating under the name of the St. Louis Transit Company.[8] As a last harangue the paper accused the governor and the state legislature of "conspiring with monopolists to consummate the game of boodle and grab by which St. Louis has been robbed of millions of dollars worth of franchises, and to coin them into a huge blanket mortgage on the streets and transportation privileges of the city." To at least a few, even at this early date, the wealth of the community, which was founded upon public property, was being absorbed by "legalized privilege" and "monopoly fiat."[9]

The news of this corporate consolidation provoked labor into its own protective form of consolidation, trade unionism. For five months after the consolidation agreement the employees of the streetcar company worked hard to increase the number of members in the Amalgamated Association of Street Railway Employees of America—Local 131. But the harder they pushed for organization, the more resistance they received from management. During the first week in March, 1900, the union submitted an ultimatum to company directors in which they demanded union recognition, the reinstatement of recently discharged union sympathizers, a ten-hour workday and the elimination of split shifts, a standard rate of wages, and a right to discuss future grievances with company directors. Edwards Whitaker, President of the St. Louis Transit Company, speaking for the other directors, publicly agreed to accept most of the union's demands, and the city of St. Louis was relieved that the threat of a major streetcar strike had been averted.[10]

Within two months it appeared that the agreement of March 10 had brought only a false sense of security to the streetcar situation in the city. On the night of April 29, the Amalgamated Association of Street Railway Employees struck the Suburban Street Railway Company, ironically the only non-consolidated line in the city. The strike on the Suburban line served as a mere prelude to the major disturbances that followed, but it was the result of the failure of protracted conferences held by the company to discuss grievances claimed by the men. The complaints were similar to those submitted to the St. Louis Transit Company six weeks before, but this time the directors refused to be "coerced." According to the strikers, the union ordered the walkout because the company had initiated a "war of extermination" against their organization, refusing to arbitrate differences and discharging employees for belonging to the union. Within a few days President Harry B. Hawes of the Police Board took the first steps to meet the crisis as he placed policemen on the Suburban cars, and allowed non-striking workers to carry their own firearms. President S. C. Jolley of the employees' union said that the men sought to win the support of the people and draw business away from the striking line. In fulfillment of these hopes the strikers appealed to St. Louisans' earlier dissatisfaction with street railway companies, and, by using hired vehicles and teams of horses, hauled passengers free of charge to a Transit Company terminus.[11]

Officials of the company might optimistically have envisioned a strike of short duration. The Suburban system was a limited access line, with opportunity of alternate travel on a nearby Transit Company line, and approximately half the employees continued to work during the strike. But on May 5, rumor began to circulate that the employees of the St. Louis Transit Company threatened to strike. The following day word came from Chairman Samuel Lee[12] of the National Executive Board of the Amalgamated Association of Street Car Employees of America that the Transit Company had not lived up to its agreement of March 10. Chairman Lee cited the non-reinstatement of discharged union men, violations of the ten-hour pact, and a general discrimination against the union as grievances and vaguely hinted that henceforth only a closed shop would be acceptable to the union. Then, on May 8, 3,325 employees of the St. Louis Transit Company went out on strike. All streetcar lines in the city were tied up. Several hundred persons who were in sympathy with the union men gathered at Thirteenth Street and Washington Avenue and "for several hours wild disorder prevailed." Participants stoned more than thirty cars, and women and children mingled with infuriated men and joined in the general demonstration.[13]

Initially the strike assumed the character of a labor versus capital issue, with the main point of contention being union recognition. On the third day of the major strike Governor Stephens came to St. Louis, met with both sides, and attempted to break the impasse. He made little progress. To the strikers the issue was unionism, though they stated that they were willing to submit all differences to a board of arbitration and abide by their decision.[14] To the Transit Company the fear of the closed shop seemed paramount, and it made offers to reinstate all former employees short of such recognition. This concession was unacceptable to the union. In Governor Stephens' mind the problem was evident, and he stated: "The whole situation is a question of unionism pure and simple."

W. D. Mahon, the union's representative, concurred and commented: "This is a fight to compel the recognition of organized labor in the city of St. Louis."[15] Both sides stood firm on principle. Management refused arbitration, while labor gave an indication of its solidarity by passing a resolution of endorsement signed by over fifty labor organizations.[16]

In many ways this class consciousness was merely the immediate manifestation of a broader citizen consciousness, which would be refined and sharpened as the effects of the strike spread to engulf the entire community. Ten days after the strike began one citizen registered his opinion of the situation, and indicated that the public also sensed an interest in the strike. He suggested that the St. Louis Transit Company, as a quasi-public concern, owed "a duty not only to those who are entitled to dividends on its stock, but to the people of the city and State as well. It occupies the public streets . . . and is the grantee of certain public franchises to be used for the benefit of the public."[17] As early as May 9, sympathizers of the strikers in many parts of the city began wearing small pieces of cardboard attached to their coat lapels, inscriptions of which read: "I will walk until the street car companies settle."[18] That small businessmen could join in the boycott, too, was indicated by the fact that eating establishments in the vicinity of the Transit Company car sheds came out in support of the strikers, refusing to furnish meals for the strikebreakers. The various labor organizations of the city organized an endless chain system in which a member would ask a friend to walk downtown with him from the residential sections of the city, boycotting the streetcar services. Each friend would, in turn, be asked to exert the same influence upon another friend, until many friends would be walking in clubs. Support in the community was so widespread that all manner of conveyance—furniture vans, carry-alls, tally-hos, milk wagons, ice wagons, sprinkling carts, hucksters' carts, and bicycles—could be seen speeding down the major streets of the city.[19] In the words of one participant, it was "very amusing at first, those that didn't walk rode in anything from a handsome carriage down to an old coal wagon. There were . . . all kinds of wagons, all *crowded*. People on horseback, on wheels, and on foot. The entire width of the street

was packed with vehicles." The *Post-Dispatch* reported that "Silk
Hats and Shirt Waists are Side by Side in Delivery Wagons and
Furniture Vans." And fashionably dressed women did not hes-
itate to climb into the homely rigs.[20]

People of different classes came increasingly to regard the
police, the "scabs," and the streetcars themselves as alien symbols of disruption to their community. Strikers and their wives
began to feel the insecurity of lost wages, businessmen the pinch
of declining sales, and consumers the inconveniences of sup-
plemental transportation and inclement weather. "Scabs" began to enter the city on May 13 and intensified animosities. The
first group of twenty-seven strikebreakers arrived in St. Louis
from towns in northern Missouri and were quartered by the
Transit Company. Three days later sixty-two additional men
were imported from Cleveland, Ohio, and the strikers could see
the beginning of a flood of replacement personnel. But "scabs"
did not know the city and compounded existing consumer
grievances. Three women traveling on a Grand Avenue car were
unsure of their location and asked the conductor for directions.
The conductor replied: "Och, we not know the streets. We can
no tell you where it is. We want your fare." When the women
informed the conductor that they did not want to pay if they
were on the wrong car, he replied: "You will please get off the
car. I know not where you go." The women were obliged to
get off the car. "That's the kind of men that are on the cars now.
They don't know what the meaning of courtesy is."[21]

As frustrations mounted, women increasingly sought to help
the strikers. Numerous women could be found in any of the
crowds that gathered, yelling as loudly as the men. When one
car passed the National Laundry, several of the women threw
bricks, tin cans, and sticks at the roof and windows of the car.
On Cass Avenue, a half-dozen women gathered to abuse the
motormen, conductors, and policemen on the passing cars. The
women would stop the cars by appearing as eager customers
and then divide up into groups of two and direct their denun-
ciations at one of the symbols of a privileged and protected corporation. One woman even tried to strike the motorman with
a dead frog tied to a string. A woman living on Easton Avenue,
not far west of Grand, saved scraps of bread for a week. Her

cook thought she was becoming very economical. The streetcars had not run on her street since the strike began, but the
day service resumed [May 16] this housewife put her scraps of
bread in the day's slop and got them soaked. As the streetcar
passed her home she ran into the street and threw the soaked
bread into the face of the non-union motorman and the emer-
gency policeman who was guarding the car. One woman undoubtedly expressed the sentiments of many St. Louisans as she
ran from a crowd and directly confronted a group of policemen
escorting a streetcar. Chief John W. Campbell, the head of the
police contingent, ordered the crowd to disperse and all did so
except the woman. "Get back or I'll have to ride over you!" cried
the police chief. "I won't," replied the woman. "I've got just as
much right on this street as you have, and I'm going to stay
here." The chief let her stay.[22]

A "citizens" committee of businessmen, alarmed by the increased violence and the disruption of trade traffic, sought to
assume the role of arbitrators between the company and the
men. When such efforts failed, some of the "leading" businessmen issued a proclamation against the strike, which only
served to convince the strikers that all capital was arrayed against
them. In commenting on this situation the editor of the *Mirror*
noted: "However the leading businessmen may feel about the
strike, the sentiment of the greater number of the people, who
are not leading businessmen, is with the strike."[23] The public
was left between two fires, wondering whom to blame, yet
asking what their own rights were in the situation.

By mid-May the strike on the Suburban line had practically
ended, differences being left for final adjustment by an arbitration board. But the promise of settlement on the Transit Company lines had completely broken down. The union had re-
laxed its closed shop demands, but stood firm for the total
reinstatement of strikers. The company, for its part, refused to
discharge any new employees. In such an atmosphere violence
increased. Sympathizers cut so many streetcar wires that General Manager George W. Baumhoff of the Transit Company was
forced to employ special detectives in an attempt to reduce such
incidents. When this action failed to bring results, the company
began to offer rewards, $100 for the arrest and conviction of

persons placing obstructions on the tracks and $250 for persons who "intimidate, throw missiles, or cut the feed wires of the St. Louis Transit Company." On other lines unruly crowds piled stones and rubbish in front of cars, despite the police, so that street department cleaning gangs could not keep the avenues cleared. A crowd of more than 1,000 persons gathered at the intersection of Seventeenth and Franklin and built a huge bonfire on the car track. Small dynamite charges were placed on the track as well. A riot call was turned in, and ten mounted policemen answered the call. With sabers drawn they charged the crowd on the sidewalks, but each time the cavalry disappeared the crowd would form again. By May 18 only 239 out of an estimated 800 cars were in operation on the city's entire transit system and many lines were closed.[24]

As street disturbances increased, many people began to see issues larger than the strike. Organized labor and St. Louis merchants had come to believe that the issue involved monopolization and corporate privilege. The combined forces of the Central Trades and Labor Union, the Building Trades Council, and the Street Railway Employees' Union issued a statement in which they, as citizens of Missouri, demanded "as much protection of the governor of the state as a corporation."[25] The strikers also formulated a statement to represent their side of the strike and to reaffirm the principle of trade unionism. To this paper the strikers were able to get the signatures of over 700 retail grocers and other retail merchants. The statement began as follows:

We recognize the principle of trades unionism as a positive, cooperative, beneficial necessity, in order to guard the interests of workingmen against the great organized power of tyrannical trusts and to prevent such trusts from crushing down wages and pauperizing the great masses of people, thereby destroying the purchasing power of our customers and injuring our business.[26]

Citizens of varying interests had come to regard the streetcar company as an alien trust and a threat to their community.

Strike sympathizers succeeded in obstructing the flow of streetcar traffic, but at the same time committed an indiscretion that allowed federal authorities to intervene. The federal government had a contract to send its mail cars over five of the St. Louis Transit Company's lines, lines disrupted by the disturbances. On May 20 Judge Elmer B. Adams of the Circuit Court issued a preliminary injunction restraining strike leaders and all other persons from interfering with the operation of the mail cars. The injunction named fifty defendants, all prominently connected with the St. Louis Street Railway Employees' Union. The injunction allowed for an increased force of deputy marshalls, or, if that proved insufficient, a posse could be sworn in to enforce the handling and delivery of the mails.[27] On May 29, 1900, eleven people were shot in South St. Louis during an encounter between armed Transit Company employees and riotous crowds. These actions convinced President Hawes of the Police Board, an active member of the city's business community, that a *posse comitatus* was necessary to "preserve order," and he directed Sheriff John H. Pohlman to place a call for 1,000 deputies—later raised to 2,500. In a striking example of coercion, service was to be compulsory and recruits were to come from the "better elements" of the city, mainly bankers, merchants, businessmen, and lawyers.[28] This unprecedented "draft" of an elite militia to defeat striking workers tested, in an interesting way, the civic consciousness of the draftees. A great many of those summoned made strenuous efforts to evade service and presented certificates from physicians to the effect that they were physically disabled. To Sheriff Pohlman it seemed as if an epidemic of sickness had broken out since the draft began. In noting that it was every citizen's duty to answer the call, the sheriff also stated that he would "not summon any citizen of Missouri outside of St. Louis. We already have too many outsiders in the city for the good of its peace."[29]

Meanwhile, the formation of the posse and the lengthening duration of the stike itself seemed to increase the solidarity of the strikers and to clarify the sympathies of the community. On May 20, 10,000 union men turned out and marched through the streets of St. Louis. Thousands of citizens lined the two-mile route and cheered the banners that prophesied the defeat of the Transit Company. One of the banners read: "I Will Break That Union If It Takes $1,000,000 To Do It—George W. Baumhoff."

On June 1, a committee of about fifty South Side residents called upon the mayor's office to complain of Transit Company employees who were carrying and discharging firearms in the neighborhoods adjacent to the company sheds. They told the mayor that unless the authorities gave them protection they would be forced to take the law into their own hands.[30]

This sentiment merely reinforced what was by then an old issue. The "saber-rattling" police, the summoned posse, and the "trigger-happy" scabs served as repeated examples of protection of corporate property, but not protection of citizens' property. The *Post-Dispatch* printed a letter to the editor signed by "A Citizen Who Loves Justice" that spoke directly to the problem. The citizen objected to having the *posse comitatus* protect the property of the Transit Company and stated: "A taxpayer is entitled to rights, but I do not think it is right to force old men to protect a company whose stock is valued at $90,000,000, for which they pay less than $40,000,000, and pay a very small tax."[31] Dr. Emil Pretorious, spokesman for a citizens group, referred to the company's men as "alien enemies, imported for the purpose of shooting down citizens of St. Louis." In denouncing them he said that the Transit Company believed that this was a government "of monopoly, by monopoly, and for monopoly." Two other members of the group declared that the taxpaying citizens were as much entitled as the Transit Company to protection for their lives and property by the police.[32]

Governor Stephens also came under public fire. His lack of initiative toward any strike settlement and his acquiescence in the utilization of police protection of corporate property led many people to hang effigies of the governor and the police authorities from poles and trolley lines on many streets. The governor blamed this anarchistic spirit on a "coterie of Democratic politicians" whom, he believed, desired to make political gains in the upcoming party primaries. "This element is sending speakers to meetings held to express sympathy for the strikers all over the city, and if not counseling disorder it is at least materially encouraging it."[33]

As the streetcar strike entered its second month, and as the anti-monopoly issue broadened its popular base of support, increased demands were placed on the state's political organiza-

tions to confront the problem directly. Realizing that the existing streetcar franchise would be difficult to overturn, the *Post-
Dispatch* placed its editorial voice behind the issue of franchise
taxation, whose popularity as an issue dated back to the late
1890s, and began to seek candidates who would work to support such an endeavor once elected to the State Board of Equalization. The newspaper began by soliciting statements on the
issue from the major Democratic candidates for office, but found
only Attorney General Crow willing to meet their request in a
positive manner. The attorney general stated that since such a
large portion of the wealth of a community consisted of intan-
gible property the state should attempt to tax such property at
its real value. He went on to note: "Whatever property is worth
for the purpose of income and sale it is worth for the purpose
of taxation . . . including therein all corporate franchises." [34]

Both major parties, long fraternally associated with business
interests, scrambled to "get right" on the tax issue. The Democratic State Convention, meeting in Kansas City on June 5, included an unequivocal declaration in favor of the taxation of
corporate franchises. According to the *Post-Dispatch*, the fight
for such taxation had been defeated in the 1899 legislature by
"trust influences," and the party was forced to take up the issue of franchise taxation because of its popularity throughout
the state. Democratic leaders realized that they must do something to counteract the original railway monopoly bill approved
by Democratic Governor Stephens, and the existing conditions
of labor troubles in St. Louis derived from that measure. [35] The
situation seemed to offer hope to the Republicans. The clearest
statement of that party's redefined position was made by the
Eighth Ward Republican Club of St. Louis which blamed cor-
rupt Democratic members of the last legislature and the political ambitions of Governor Stephens for the "gigantic street railway trust" that had "plundered," "oppressed," and "harrassed"
the citizens of St. Louis. One other local political organization
was active. Known as the Franchise Repeal Association, this
group held mass meetings to discuss the possibilities of municipal ownership and urged the Municipal Assembly to repeal
franchises held by corporate interests. [36]

The most violent episode of the strike occurred on June 10,

when three men were killed and fourteen wounded in an alter-
cation between marching strikers and the sheriff's posse. The
persistent violence and the inability of the union to reach an
agreement with the Transit Company finally induced American
Federation of Labor President Samuel Gompers to come to the
city to try his hand at persuasion. But Gompers failed where
others had failed. The company stood firm in its refusal to reinstate former employees if it meant the dismissal of men then in
service. Gompers, his pride undoubtedly hurt, signed a declaration of a general boycott against the Transit Company. In addition to this the Central Trades and Labor Union organized its
own bus line, funded by subscriptions, and placed over twenty
vehicles in service. But after two months of the strike the union
began to weaken. Donations to the strike fund were no longer
adequate to maintain worker subsistence, the union bus company was unable to pay its own way, and popular sentiment,
itself growing tired of the strike, favored some sort of compromise settlement. The Transit Company seemed to have things
going its way, except for the persistence of the boycott. According to the *Mirror*, "North and South End people refused to
ride in the cars, even though all violence had ceased."[37]

On July 2, 1900, after two weeks of quiet negotiations, a conference between the strikers' grievance committee and company representatives reached a tentative "compromise" settlement that, in actuality, meant defeat for the union on all crucial
issues. The provisions of the agreement included: rates of pay
and hours of service to be the same as on March 10, 1900; employees to be free to join or not to join the union; a company
commitment to listen to all complaints; and vacancies to be filled
by men from a union list of strikers only. This last point made
the agreement palatable to the strikers, and with it the Street
Railway Union at a mass meeting endorsed the action of its executive committee. This agreement lasted less than one week,
when union leaders ordered a renewal of the strike and boycott. This action came after the union learned that the Transit
Company had hired non-union men in violation of their agreement. The union continued its strike until, admitting defeat, it
finally called off the boycott and accepted the reality that many
strikers had been effectively blacklisted.[38]

Aside from the union's defeat, efforts to repeal the streetcar franchise ordinance in St. Louis failed in the Municipal Assembly, and Attorney General Crow's efforts in the state courts met a similar fate. The attorney general initiated action to annul the consolidation of the street railway companies, accused the Transit Company of stock watering, and brought proceedings in the state supreme court to revoke the charters of both the St. Louis Transit and United Railways Companies. His actions lingered on the court calendar and were ultimately dismissed in early 1901.[39] The State Board of Equalization also refused to increase the taxes due quasi-public corporations in the state even though 40,000 voters signed a petition in favor of such reform.[40]

Urban consumers also did not appear to have received any of the efficient, modern improvements promised by the consolidated transit network. The boosters of consolidation had promised improved transportation, an easing of downtown congestion, and a transfer system. But the service was not greatly improved and the mayor's office received numerous complaints from the public in 1901. Mayor Rolla Wells was himself a witness:

Several protesting delegations called on me in the City Hall, bitterly complaining that frequently, large numbers of persons were left standing at the street intersections in the shivering cold as cars rapidly passed them by without stopping. Often stones were hurled by angry citizens at the cars speeding by. The spokesmen were vehement in denouncing the service.

To personally inform myself . . . I visited some of the street corners and intersections, and closely observed the service and watched the waiting, indignant groups, and saw for myself that there were good grounds for the popular uproar.[41]

A similar example involved an incident on a Laclede Avenue streetcar months after the collapse of the strike. The conductor of the car had allowed a woman passenger to be carried three blocks beyond her proper destination. Upon notice of this the woman became somewhat perturbed and the following dialogue ensued:

Lady: "You are a novice and a bungler, or a man who does wrong with malice aforethought."

Conductor: "Don't keep this car waiting, madam. We have a schedule
on this system. . . . "

Lady: "Of course you have a schedule. You have a plant, a management, a gridiron layout of tracks, rolling stock, attorneys, adjusters,
motormen, conductors, and a schedule. It must be maintained if
everything else goes to the wall. The schedule is the unrivaled fe-
tich. You see that I read the papers, and I have stood on the corners
scores of times to be passed by, a sacrifice to the schedule."

Other occupants of the streetcar came to the woman's assistance and forced the conductor to flag a passing streetcar and
arrange for her a transfer that would carry her back those three
blocks. The woman could not help but give a parting shot to
St. Louis' symbol of corporate efficiency and stated: "If I've
broken that schedule I'll enjoy New Year's a great deal better
than I had hoped to."[42]
     There were, however, many positive aspects that evolved from
the streetcar strike in St. Louis. The strike developed a cross-
class sense of community consciousness that was in many cases
as remarkable as the examples of worker solidarity. People in
roles as consumers, housewives, workers, taxpayers, citizens,
and merchants united against the streetcar monopoly. The success of the boycott was probably the major inducement forcing
the company to agree to the settlement of July 2. The strike also
brought into focus questions concerning municipal services,
corporate arrogance, legislative corruption, franchise taxation,
and municipal ownership that people, though conscious of, had
not united behind in a call for reform. The Democratic legislature of 1901 did pass a watered-down franchise tax law[43] that
many Democrats, though not proud of, were at least relieved
to have enacted. State Senator George T. Lee of Carter County
stated: "I am mighty glad the assembly passed a franchise bill.
I would hardly have dare[d] to go home if it had not."[44] The
intense feeling against the railway trust also greatly contributed
to the showing of mayoral candidate Lee Meriwether who, while
running on a municipal ownership ticket in the 1901 campaign,
polled approximately 28 percent of the vote in St. Louis.[45] And
probably the subtlest, but most important, result of the strike
was the election of labor attorney Joseph W. Folk to the posi-

tion of St. Louis Circuit Attorney. From this position Folk went on to prosecute the boodle and bribery investigations that involved those same street railway corporations and the St. Louis Municipal Assembly. These investigations won Folk popular support, national recognition, and eventually the governorship as a progressive reformer.

The St. Louis streetcar strike, as a case study, exhibits a complex interaction of opposing forces in a rapidly changing urban-industrial environment. Most St. Louisans appeared to accept the demands of the strikers as legitimate labor grievances, and realized the absolute control the company had over its workers. When the corporation refused to arbitrate and bargain collectively, it was met by an expression of labor solidarity within the city, and the strike assumed the character of a class conflict. But it was a consumer struggle as well. Complaints of inefficient and discourteous service, unsafe operations, tax inequities, and trust control of a necessary public conveyance quickly converted the strike into a community action. People altered their lifestyles and everyday patterns to support the boycott by walking or by taking alternative forms of transportation. The Transit Company, as the antisocial product of a legislative monopoly and the symbol of corporate modernization, actually caused the emotions of producers and consumers to merge. Class and sex distinctions blurred and the "public welfare" became paramount. People actively resisted alien forces that threatened their community in the form of "foreign" stockholders, armed strikebreakers, and police support of the corporation. A quasi-public corporation operated in defiance of the public interest. As a part of a larger process of corporate growth and modernization, private concerns seemed to place themselves above their public obligations. St. Louisans were part of an even larger public to which the terms "trust" and "monopoly" had come to have sinister connotations. To many, the rewards of modernization were not worth the sacrifices demanded. People, as the strike demonstrated, rejected imposition in the form of corporate consolidation and demanded that their rights and privileges be recognized and protected.

POPULAR REACTION AND INVESTIGATION OF THE BEEF TRUST

St. Louisans had confronted the monopolization of an essential service during the transit strike of 1900. As consumers, they expressed concern for the way in which the streetcar service operated, and as voters and taxpayers, for the corresponding issue of franchise taxation. As citizens, their interests turned to franchise privileges and the police protection granted to the corporation. As workers, they focused their attention on unionization and working conditions, and the refusal of the company to accept arbitration. But in their daily lives people also had to contend with the age-old problem of making means and ends meet.

When President William McKinley ran a successful campaign for reelection in 1900 on a slogan that promised the American worker a "full-dinner pail," he indeed appeared optimistic. Perhaps more people were working and the worst aspects of the depression had passed, but severe fluctuations in the cost of living and retail price indexes created a more dreary picture. From 1891 through 1897, real hourly earnings in all industries remained almost stationary, and from 1898 through 1902 they rose only slightly. But after falling 9 percent for 1891–1897, the cost of living index ominously pushed upward after 1898. By 1902 it had increased 9 percent above the 1898 level. Similar results appeared in the retail price index for food. For 1891–1897, food prices dropped 5.2 percent, but in 1898–1902, they actually jumped 8.3 percent.[1] Prosperity had not come to rural and urban America, but to corporate America. Such changes created problems of serious consequence. The director of the Board of Charity of St. Joseph, Missouri, worried that monthly grants of money, usually not more than $5.00 per family, would soon be inadequate to meet rising food prices. The cheapest kind of beef had increased in cost from 5 cents a pound to 12 1/2 cents a pound in just one year. Potatoes had more than doubled in price in a year from 40 to 50 cents to $1.05 a bushel. According to the director, an allotment which had once been good for the purchase of twenty pounds of soup meat and two bushels of potatoes would now have to be stretched to buy twelve pounds of meat and one bushel of potatoes.[2]

As price increases continued during the "trust era" which began in 1898, people, in their roles as consumers, increasingly pointed the finger of blame at the trusts. They sought their own means of meeting the problem through consumer boycotts and popular pressure for legal action. Consumers understood their declining purchasing power to be directly linked to corporate consolidation or, in the term most commonly used at the time, the trusts. Over 100 trusts were incorporated during 1899 alone, more than doubling the number in existence prior to that time. By 1903, the number had increased to over 300.[3]

People struggled to grasp the connection between rising prices and corporate consolidation. Occasionally, newspapers helped. The *St. Louis Post-Dispatch*, in August, 1899, found prices higher on nearly every necessity of life. In fact, the cost of these necessities, on the average, proved 15 percent higher than they had been a year earlier. This trend occurred at a time of plentiful crops, when the supply of raw materials of all kinds had never been larger, and when the amount of manufactured products exceeded previous years. These facts called into question presumed "laws" of supply and demand. The *Post-Dispatch* concluded that, without unnatural manipulation, these conditions would cause a decrease in prices instead of an increase. But the trusts had forced price increases upon the people to "make dividends for largely over-capitalized combinations."[4] In some instances, such as with the Beef Trust, the large slaughtering houses linked price increases to shortages in cattle. But butchers and consumers refused to accept these explanations. Price advances forced many butchers out of business,

especially in the poorer urban sections of the city where demand declined. Butchers blamed the increase on price-fixing by
the large packing concerns, and consumers easily accepted these
assertions when they learned that the price of cattle had gone
up 5 percent while consumer prices had advanced an average
of 33 percent.[5] High beef prices in St. Louis in 1899 caused consumer pressures and butcher dissatisfaction with the trust. The
situation provoked retail butchers in the city to follow preliminary plans drawn by the National Retail Butchers' Cooperative
Association, to erect cooperative slaughterhouses and sell to
subscribers directly.[6]

Consumers and butchers appeared justified in their suspicions. By the turn of the century the Beef Trust possessed economic power over an industry exceeded only in extent by the
Standard Oil Trust. Gustavas Swift had combined refrigerated
railroad cars and refrigerated warehouses to create the first national meat-packing company in the late 1880s. Other packing
houses quickly followed his example and soon formed a system based on a mutuality of interest. About 1885 these major
meat packers, especially the Armour, Swift, and Morris concerns, combined their efforts. They formed a pool to dominate
a large portion of the food industry by controlling and regulat-
ing shipments of dressed meats to the markets. By 1893, the
packers had expanded their combination. For the next three
years, representatives of cooperating companies met weekly on
Tuesday to divide the country into territories and determine the
volume of shipments each house could make for that week. The
combine worked well and, by 1898, had expanded to include
six leading companies. They shared statistical reports and pro-
portioned shipments on that basis. Any company exceeding its
percentage of shipments paid a 40–cent (later 75–cent) fine per
hundred pounds of excess. Companies short of their quotas received this fee as compensation. A group of auditors kept a check
on the system. To complete the arrangement, the pool adopted
a uniform method of figuring the cost of fresh meat so that profit
margins would remain identical. This pooling agreement continued in undisturbed form until the spring of 1902.[7]

Producers, not consumers, initiated the first protests against

the meat-packing industry. The Beef Trust maintained tight secrecy about its pooling agreements, but its activities aroused the
suspicions of Western cattlemen and butchers. In response to
complaints from these groups, a special committee of U.S. senators from Missouri, Kansas, Illinois, Texas, and Nebraska began hearings in St. Louis in November of 1888, to investigate
the industry. The senators selected St. Louis because the International Cattle Range Association and the Butchers' National
Protective Association met there. After two years of investigation the committee issued the Vest Report of 1890. It confirmed
the existence of a "Beef Trust" which included the Armour,
Swift, Morris, and Hammond companies. The committee found
convincing proof of collusion in the price fixing of beef, the division of territory and business, including public contracts, and
the compulsion of retailers to purchase from the major packers.
Conditions revealed by the Vest Report helped facilitate the
passage of the Sherman Antitrust Act on July 2, 1890. Livestock
producers, alarmed over low stock prices, prompted a federal
grand jury to hold hearings in 1895. However, it brought no
indictments.[8]

By the turn of the century, anger at the Beef Trust may have
attracted readers to H. G. Wells' story, "When the Sleeper
Wakes," which told of a universal food trust. When the people
came under the food trust, the slot machine lunch would be
universal. On the walls above the machines, mottos would direct: "Help Yourself," "No Tips," and "Be Your Own Waiter."
The trust's first economy would put all waiters out of work. Of
necessity, consumers would take what the trust's slot machine
offered or go hungry. This very well might be meatless sand-
wiches, chicory coffee, oleo butter, and other articles, "that a
trust may put before its customers so as to secure dividends for
its stockholders." Consumers found it useless to smash the slot
lunch machine, "as a man does not quarrel with his bread and
oleo." After all, the trust might forget to refill the machines![9]

Fear of a food trust, control of meat products, and rising consumer costs increased in November, 1901. Reports surfaced that
certain Chicago dealers had combined to corner the egg market. The large packing houses entered the chicken killing busi-

ness, bought eggs in enormous amounts, and placed them in cold storage for speculative purposes. One would-be poet contemplated the results as he put his thoughts to rhyme:

Now the gentle egglet seeketh
For admission to the trust,
And it sayeth (loud it speaketh);
Lemme in there, or I'll bust;
I, too long have lingered lowly
At a dime or two a doz.;
Now I seek a higher goal, a
Taller price than used to wuz
At a dollar a doz., the waiter
Will no longer yell "Ham and";
I'll be brother to the tater,
As to price, and rule the land.[10]

A common rumor spread that greedy packing corporations busily worked hens overtime, feeding them red pepper and raw meat to stimulate their laying power. Reportedly in four and one-half months, Chicago's big cold storage houses of Armour and Swift gained control of 500,000 cases of eggs, enough to manipulate prices.[11] As long as prices increased moderately, or high levels did not continue for extended periods of time, consumers remained cynical commentators and sporadic grumblers. As temporarily shown with beef in St. Louis in 1899, however, consumers and butchers could potentially unite to confront the trust.

News of exorbitant price increases for beef frequented newspapers during the first months of 1902, telling consumers what they already knew. According to the *St. Joseph Gazette*, people of moderate means severely felt the recent advance in nearly all food products. Along with the increased cost, few of them had experienced a corresponding increase in their annual incomes. Supposedly, the country experienced a period of "unexampled prosperity," but curiously, it seemed restricted to certain corporations and trusts. If the Beef Trust had advanced meat prices only a fraction of a cent, claims of shortages might have been accepted without challenge. Advances of from three to four cents a pound seemed to stretch credibility.[12] The *Lamar Leader* determined that, with the price of beef "soaring among the clouds" and the manufacturers of tinware forming a trust, the average workman would find the promised "full-dinner pail" to be "chimerical."[13] The editor of the *St. Joseph Daily News* noted that four straight years of price increases had forced the poor to quit using all but the cheaper grades of beef. Market butchers blamed the price elevation on a conspiracy of packers. They asserted that the rise in the price of dressed meat appeared well out of proportion to the increase in the price of cattle.[14]

Packers and consumers also differed in their explanations of rising beef costs and the effects of those costs upon people. The major beef packers claimed that conditions required the advance in meat prices. In their defense the packers pointed to a light corn crop, caused by drought, which had raised the price of cattle feed. They also accused farmers of holding out for higher prices which, linked to the growing consumer demand, made the cost of beef dear to consumers.[15] Charles W. Armour, head of the Armour Packing Company, repeatedly denied knowledge of a Beef Trust. He maintained that "natural causes" led to expensive dressed meats and livestock. In fact, the workingmen need not fear increased costs. Armour contended that: "The man who lives on prime rib roasts and porterhouse steaks pays for the advance in the price of beef, while the price to the purchasers for cheaper cuts is kept down."[16] Such statements made no sense at all to the editors of the *St. Louis Labor Compendium*. They responded that "the most unpopular man these days is he who tries to prove there is no meat trust."[17] George Marr, an agent for Armour and Company in Houston, Texas, supported his employer when he spoke of the effects of high meat prices on the workingman. In Marr's opinion, the appetites of workingmen did not suit their resources. The average worker with a wage of $2 or $3 a day "wants porterhouse, demands porterhouse and, in the past, has been able to get porterhouse because the market was easy and within reach of his purse."[18]

Working people held a different view. Alios Bilker, a St. Louis Street Department sweeper, earned $1.50 a day and voiced his own opinion of the meat situation:

We have meat but once a day now at our house. It is too high to expect a poor man to serve it at every meal. As long as I have had a family I do not know when it was so high. Nowadays we buy round steak, cut as thin as paper almost, for twenty cents or perhaps fifteen cents, and we are lucky in getting it at that. Generally we have to buy shoulder and neck pieces, because we get more of that part of the cow for the money. We have to fall back on beans and cheap things to take the place of meat. There is much grumbling down in my neighborhood around Geyer Avenue. We all believe that a few rich men get together and make the prices. That story about higher beef and scarcity of corn and so on may do for some, but we do not believe that it is necessary to send up the price of meat the way they do.[19]

The assumed inability of workers to purchase select cuts of meat concealed a powerlessness to purchase a sufficient quantity of meat or any meat at all.

The federal government offered a strange kind of assistance. H. W. Wiley, head of the Bureau of Chemistry of the United States Agriculture Department, encouraged the adoption of cereal substitutes for high-priced beef products. Only half-jokingly, he predicted that vegetarianism might become a fad if beef prices continued to soar.[20] The editor of the *Baltimore American* joked along similar lines. Linking production and consumption, he put his suggestion to rhyme:

Mary had a little lamb,
    With mintsauce on the side;
When Mary saw the meat trust's bill,
    It shocked her so she cried.

Mary had a little veal—
    A cutlet, nicely broiled.
Her papa, to pay for that veal,
    All morning sorely toiled.

Mary had a little steak—
    A porterhouse quite small,
And when the bill came in, she sighed;
    No dress for me next fall.

Mary had a little roast—
    As juicy as could be—
And Mary's papa simply went
    Right into bankruptcy.

Mary isn't eating meat;
  She has a better plan;
She vows it's ladylike to be
  A vegetarian.[21]

A more graphic story involved a seventeen-year-old boy who attempted suicide with morphine. When asked the reason for his near fatal attempt, the boy replied that he had to support his mother and sister on his wages of $7 a week. He earned that sum setting type, but had lost his job the previous week. He then found work as a pantry boy at the Westmorland Hotel. But "my earnings would not meet our expenses. Meat was so high and all the world seemed against me. So I decided to die."[22] To consumers living on the margins of survival, the slightest increase in food prices could be catastrophic.

In mid-April, 1902, the precipitous rise in meat prices and popular dissatisfaction prompted mild action from the attorney general's office. On April 14, U.S. Attorney General Philander C. Knox instructed William Warner, U.S. District Attorney in Kansas City, to take preliminary steps to investigate the so-called Beef Trust.[23] Traffic officials of Eastern and Western railroads added to the problems of the major packing houses. They asserted that plans to corner the beef market had been implemented in Chicago. They based this belief on the fact that beef provisions destined for export had rapidly declined in the last month. The export figure appeared smaller than at any time in the past several years. The not-so-subtle hint by those officials suggested stockpiling by large packing houses for speculative purposes.[24]

Missourians, like other citizens, raised many questions concerning the ethics of the meat-packing industry. One Missouri stockman found no excuse for the "squeeze" in beef prices. In his opinion the packers were the people who were making the money from the recent increases in the price of meat. While stockmen were getting good prices for their cattle, feed remained high, making the cost of feeding higher than it had been. This stockman could only conclude that "the packers' raise is way out of proportion to the increase in the price of cattle. The big fat steers which can be bought for 6 cents a pound now have not been below 5 cents for the past five years. It is certainly hard on the common people."[25] The *Springfield Leader and Dem-ocrat* also raised questions concerning the sale of beef in Mis-souri. Located in the heart of the drought section, dealers in Springfield, Missouri, somehow could sell beef a good deal cheaper than dealers in Kansas City, the state's leading cattle market and slaughterhouse center. Some cuts sold in Kansas City at almost twice the price they did in Springfield. What possible explanation could be given? Charges for delivery ser-vice, supply depots, and wagons proved comparable, and Kan-sas City packers even had to pay railroad duties to ship to the southern part of the state. The *Leader-Democrat* concluded that the only explanation lay in the type of business conducted. Springfield packers had competition, and the Kansas City trust did not. Many local Springfield butchers continued to do their own killing. In most other places, the packers had forced the butchers to quit killing by establishing their own local meat market outlets. According to a Springfield newspaper: "That was never done here, and old-fashioned ways still prevail to an ex-tent in the butchers' trade."[26] The reading public slowly re-ceived a lesson in trust policy and pocketbook economics. In addition, they realized the threat to their nearly self-sufficient lifestyle and values of economic independence.

Many people began to fear the formation of an even greater food trust from within the Beef Trust. The Retail Butchers and Meat Dealers' Protective Association also condemned the meat combine for the "almost prohibitive" prices of meat. Members alerted consumers that trust control might extend to foodstuffs in general. J. A. Hoffman, second vice president of the orga-nization, commented that the Beef Trust had taken advantage of the fact of a natural cause for the rise in beef and now used it as a lever to artificially advance the price of meats. He then warned consumers that the Beef Trust was not content merely to run up the price of meat beyond reason, "it is also control-ling, to a great extent, the vegetable market. The price of po-tatoes is today regulated by this same Beef Trust . . . . Butter and eggs are not beyond the grasp of this same trust."[27] In one week, Swift and Company reportedly rushed 100,000 cases of eggs into cold storage for speculative purposes. The *St. Louis Chronicle*, on April 23, 1902, reported that 50,000 cases of eggs had been stored by St. Louis speculators endeavoring to force up the price of eggs three cents in one week. A day later, the *Kansas City Star* reported that major packers were uniting to control the supply of eggs and poultry. It also claimed to possess information that major packers bought directly from the farmers, thereby shutting out the concession men. Eggs, which sold at 10 cents a dozen in 1901, sold for 18 cents a dozen in April, 1902.[28]

On April 19, 1902, reporters for the *Kansas City Journal* informed their readers that the Beef Trust intended to corner all food products and form a colossal food combination. Readers, as consumers, feared the dream of H. G. Wells might be possible. Reportedly, citizens of Philadelphia and other Eastern cities had already realized the Beef Trust's power in the butter, egg, and poultry line, and feared a similar corner of the vegetable and fruit market. Allegedly, the big packing firms had been anticipating the formation of one gigantic trust for some time. As a result, the various concerns had increased plant capacities which would enhance profits in the event of a trust agreement. Plant expansion had increased cold storage room beyond storage needs. With the surplus space, the packers could control the cold storage facilities of every great market and buy up provisions to hold until a corner could be effected.[29] Exorbitant price figures appeared on every kind of perishable food preserved in a refrigerator. Spring chickens that had been killed in 1901, wrapped up in "trust tissue paper" and laid away by carloads in cold storage plants, sold at a cost far greater than 1902 broilers. Apparently the Beef Trust held back all food supplies to create a "ficticious scarcity" that would assure higher prices. The *Mirror* reported: "The man who eats broilers and truffles and the man who pampers his family on pot-roast and cabbage, are at one in their grievance against the beef trust."[30]

In many cities consumers began expressing attitudes of resistance to what they regarded as trust imposition. Although the advance in the cost of meat to consumers had not proven a conspiracy, "an impression of this kind could result in nothing else than general agitation and resentment."[31] In the smaller St. Louis meat shops, butchers found their customers "complaining lustily." In the city, the consumption of meat fell off 5 percent in two weeks. Fish became the staple for many as the demand trebled. Butchers and consumers began to unite to resist the "extortion" of the Beef Trust. In the words of one retail butcher: "Our interests are the same as those of the public." This same butcher noted that consumers had begun to advocate cooperative butcher shops, "like those started in New York by butchers to fight the trust."[32] In Indiana, Indianapolis grocers, who had conducted meat business for years, discontinued the sale of beef and beef products. They notified suppliers that they would not resume the trade until they witnessed a "substantial" reduction in prices. Several butcher shops also closed or refused to buy from Chicago packers. In some instances the boycott caused butchers to contemplate cooperative resistance in which they would buy live cattle and do their own slaughtering.[33]

Workers yielded to their roles as consumers and used their producer-oriented forms of organization to boycott the trust. In Bloomington, Illinois, 2,000 employees of the Chicago and Alton Railroad shops agreed that none of their members would eat meat for a thirty-day period. The workers hoped to encourage others to follow their example and force the Beef Trust to reduce the prices of meat. Dayton, Ohio, protestants started an endless chain letter crusade against the Beef Trust. Thousands of letters broadcasted the high price of meat and encouraged abstinence for one week. Four hundred workers in Bellefontaine, Ohio, signed an agreement refusing to eat any meat for thirty days. The Central Labor Union of Amsterdam, New York, composed of twenty-five subordinate unions and 5,000 members, began a thirty-day boycott to abstain from using any meat handled by the so-called "meat trust."[34]

Popular outcry against the Beef Trust and the notice of potential federal litigation provoked legal action in Missouri. On April 29, 1902, Missouri Attorney General Crow filed a petition with Chief Justice Gavon D. Burgess of the state supreme court. Crow requested representatives of the major packing houses in Missouri to testify concerning the alleged Beef Trust's control of meat prices. He based his petition on violations of the state's antitrust law which prohibited packers from conspiring to fix the wholesale and retail prices of all beef, pork, and dressed meats. Judge Burgess complied with the order and asked representatives to appear before the court on May 6, 1902.[35] Crow noted that federal authorities had instituted suits against the Beef Trust but would not hear any evidence for some time. He remarked that his investigation would be the first in the country to reveal the real conditions among the packers. The attorney general had spent six weeks researching the causes for the current high meat prices before filing his petition. He noted that the investigation was "arousing interest throughout the country."[36]

On May 6, 1902, "Beef Trust" hearings began in Jefferson City before the Missouri Supreme Court. None of the representatives from the packing companies appeared. Their legal counsel had advised him to object to the hearings by questioning the constitutionality of the antitrust law.[37] The court also subpoenaed more than forty retail butchers from St. Louis, Kansas City, and St. Joseph. They did appear and told of trust methods in those cities. These butchers testified that the "Big Four"—Armour, Swift, Cudahy, Morris—fixed a uniform price for meat and fined their agents, salesmen, or companies if they sold at a lower price.[38] Some butchers testified that they received rebates on purchases, some in cash and others in an extra supply of meat. Packing-house salesmen had cautioned them to keep the dealings secret. They levied fines if others found out. This tightly controlled system, including a blacklist of delinquent creditors, forced butchers to buy from the Big Four packers or fear a boycott by the combine.[39]

The second day of the inquiry revealed further evidence of the combine's efforts to control prices. Testimony showed that salesmen of Swift, Armour, Morris, and other large concerns undersold the smaller packing companies, with the intention of driving them out of business.[40] Retail butchers felt similar trust pressure. Maurice Prendiville, a St. Louis butcher, stated that Armour damaged the interests of some butchers by operating delivery wagons and selling to customers direct and at a prohibitively lower price. Evidently designed as a lesson, the practice taught butchers to buy only "trust" beef and at a regular fixed price. Even shippers appeared at the mercy of the combine. If shippers did not sell all their goods to the trust, it would refuse to make any purchase, whatsoever. If a shipper refused their price and chose to reship his meat to Chicago, he faced similar results. The packers merely wired their offer to Chicago and the shipper would receive the same price there.[41]

Testimony not only confirmed that the trust artificially increased meat prices, but it also forced consumers to purchase an inferior product. According to one St. Louis meat dealer, "the number of cattle sold and killed in East St. Louis this season has been unusually large." He quickly noted that most of that meat had been placed in cold storage and withheld from the market. When the public learned that the big packers had sold diseased meat to St. Louis consumers, the term "concession" beef entered the consumer's vocabulary. Under this practice wholesalers sold "ripe," "aged," "stale," or "beginning to spoil" meat to butchers at a reduced price, after the packing firms granted a price concession to the wholesaler. During the hearings, Captain T. L. O'Sullivan, a St. Louis meat dealer, under oath, revealed the sale of decayed meat in that city. It had been rubbed to remove "whiskers," painted to restore a wholesome color, and preserved with ammonia. "Lumpy-jawed" cattle, condemned by government inspectors in East St. Louis, were smuggled over the bridge at night and sold in the St. Louis market at a discount as concession beef. These revelations prompted public attention on several fronts. The St. Louis House of Delegates considered measures to provide for the proper inspection of cattle. Mayor Rolla Wells and Health Commissioner Dr. Max C. Starkloff held a conference and decided to add three additional meat inspectors.[42]

Following these exposures the state's legal apparatus began to respond. The selling of life-threatening adulturated meat provoked Circuit Attorney Joseph W. Folk to initiate his own investigation. Folk requested the St. Louis grand jury to proceed against the Beef Trust and stated: "This has become a subject for the criminal courts and the matter will be investigated as have been the bribery scandals, and I have no doubt but that men who have been selling diseased and decayed meat to St. Louisans will be landed behind the bars of the penitentiary."[43] The same feeling prompted Attorney General Edward C. Crow to indicate that he meant not merely to break up the combine

charging outrageous prices, but also to force the packers to furnish better meat. Confident that ample evidence had been obtained, on May 10, Crow asked for a writ of ouster against the
major meat-packing firms in the state. He alleged violations of
the antitrust laws of Missouri. In the writ the attorney general
charged that a combine of packing companies owned, controlled, and supplied at fixed prices to the general public, 90
percent of all the meat sold in Missouri. The Missouri investigation received national attention.[44] U.S. District Attorney William Warner of Kansas City, speaking for U.S. Attorney General Philander C. Knox, asked to procure a copy of the evidence
obtained by Crow for use in the federal government investigation.[45]

The information revealed by the Missouri investigation, the
anticipation of federal and state actions elsewhere, increased
newspaper comment, and the persistent high beef cost all served
to intensify popular reaction. At Lynn, Massachusetts, nearly
1,700 employees of the General Electric Company, representing
at least 4,000 consumers, formed an anti-beefeating league.
Members pledged to abstain from beef consumption for thirty
days, and promoters expected 5,000 company employees to join
before the boycott ended. In Middletown, New York, 300
members of the Laborer's Union voted unanimously to abstain
from Western beef for one month. The Central Labor Union in
Portland, Maine, unanimously adopted a resolution protesting
the advance in meat prices and organized a similar thirty-day
boycott. In Topeka, Kansas, 2,500 Sante Fe Railroad shop employees began a thirty-day beef boycott and caused an immediate 50 percent drop in meat sales in the working-class sections of the city. The continued high beef prices in St. Joseph,
Missouri, and Omaha, Nebraska, caused consumers to switch
to a fish diet. And in New York City angry Jewish consumers
actually conducted a spontaneous food riot, while 500 Jewish
men and women met and formed the Ladies Anti-Beef Trust
Association. The Association threatened to start its own cooperative stores if the price of kosher meat did not come down.[46]

These consumer attempts to discipline the Beef Trust succeeded. As soon as beef reached prohibitive price levels, the
consumption fell off. People simply stopped eating meat.

Thousands of small meat shops closed, and the public responded by substituting cereal foods for meat. In the opinion of one editor, people stopped eating eggs when dealers pushed the price too high. They also cut down on butter, sugar, and coffee in the same manner, and under the same circumstances. They then "revolted and they stopped eating meat . . . when their common sense told them that the prices asked were asked only because the beef barons thought they had the supply so thoroughly cornered that they could charge anything they pleased."[47] An indication that the packers felt consumer pressure appeared in mid-May, 1902, when beef prices stabilized. In the opinion of local butchers this action resulted from popular agitation and legal prosecutions.[48]

In addition to the reactions to price fixing, trade restraints, and corporate arrogance, some individuals questioned corporate consolidation itself. The Beef Trust's ability to control the butcher and small farmer, and dictate costs to consumers, resulted from unchecked corporate consolidation. As one labor leader suggested: "It seems probable that a new era will distinguish the lives of farmers when the food trust gets the nation absolutely organized and systematized."[49] In earlier days a farmer living near a small town might have had a calf, hog, or young steer for sale. He probably would have taken his animal to the local butcher. The butcher paid him a fair price, slaughtered the animal, and sold the meat at reasonable prices to his customers. But things had changed. Agents of the Beef Trust watched the local butcher, and, if they found him trading independently, they became concerned. They required the local butcher to buy all his meat from the trust. If he refused, the trust would cut off his regular supply of pork, mutton, veal, or beef. The local farmer could only supply on occasion, but the butcher needed supplies daily. These conditions forced the butcher to curtail his trade with the farmer and buy from the trust, while the farmer had to sell his stock to the trust or keep them himself. Even when the butcher dealt with the trust, other worries remained. The old-fashioned methods of many small retail butchers placed them at a distinct disadvantage. Butchers experienced difficulty competing with larger, modern concerns that operated more efficiently and utilized every part of the slaughtered animal. Thus, consumers confronted the final result, purchasing trust-made products at trust-made prices.[50]

Many people did not regard this "modernizing" process as just, and they resisted its implications. Reverend George Lloyd, pastor of the Church of the Redeemer in St. Louis, expressed these feelings well in a sermon:

Combination and centralization, they tell us, are the mark of the age; that we can not help ourselves; that in a big age big combinations of manufacturers and purveyors are facilitated by a marvelous development in rapid transit. Such reasoning is faulty, inasmuch as it takes for granted that what is naturally expected to be is right, without considering its character and its effect on people.[51]

Citizens, as consumers, taxpayers, workers, and housewives, recognized the larger forces pressing down upon them. They understood the "us-and-them" relationship to "the interests," and reacted against those perceptions.

On June 28, 1902, The Missouri Supreme Court acted on Attorney General Crow's request for ouster proceedings against the Beef Trust in Missouri. The court appointed I. H. Kinley of Kansas City as a special commissioner to gather further testimony. Kinley finally filed his report on January 3, 1903. He confirmed the earlier findings of Crow that certain companies had entered a combine in Missouri to regulate the price of meats. A week later attorneys for the packers filed exceptions to the report of the commissioner, but to no avail.[52] Finally, on March 20, 1903, the Missouri Supreme Court awarded judgment to the state against the Armour, Hammond, Cudahy, Swift, and Schwarzschild and Sulzberger packing companies. Fined $5,000 plus court costs, each of the five Missouri packing companies was required to pay within thirty days or be ousted from the state. By April 12, 1903, all defendants had complied with the order. Drafts totaling $27,136 reached the state supreme court.[53]

The struggle against the Beef Trust drew upon a tradition that stressed the need to preserve the economic independence of an individual in a democratic society. Farmers knew the reason for disappearing local butchers. Butchers also realized why they were being forced out of business, and consumers recognized who dictated the prices of their goods. People did not live by bread alone but by meat as well, and rising meat prices placed severe stress on limited family budgets. Conscious of their situation, citizens ably formulated their own responses. They sensed their sacrifice to a larger process of corporate modernization, and they resisted. Consumers altered their diet, stopped eating meat, and participated in formal, organized boycotts. They also realized that some manner of control was needed, as trusts had placed themselves beyond the law and apart from society. Popular actions forced the judicial system to respond. Investigations at the state level, such as the one in Missouri, exposed corporate arrogance which, in turn, deepened consumer indignation. These investigations not only served as examples for national policymakers, but also as expressions of popular reaction to economic consolidation.

A COMMUNITY CONFRONTS THE BEEF TRUST: THE CHICAGO TEAMSTERS' STRIKE OF 1902

In the Spring of 1902 a teamsters' strike broke out against the major packing houses in Chicago, a strike that had shocking effects on the people of that city. What made this labor dispute so volatile and almost instantly explosive, was the manner in which it merged with the undercurrent of popular indignation against the Beef Trust. The teamsters' strike itself, the possibility that other related unions would go out in support of the drivers, and the threat that all trade in meat would be halted in the city of Chicago, created a tense situation. However, the Chicago teamsters' strike was "much aggravated . . . by the recent advances in the price of meats, and by the newspaper disclosures indicating that the advances were due to efforts on the part of the packers, working through a combination or trust, to get larger profits for themselves."[1] Beef prices had been climbing sharply during the first five months of 1902, and newspapers had been devoting front-page coverage to the recent federal investigation of the meat-packing industry and to a similar investigation already in progress at the state level in Missouri.[2]

The actions of the Beef Trust, part of a larger process of corporate consolidation and control over the market, directly threatened the popular conception of traditional rights and customs. The sense that there were proper economic actions and social obligations within society seemed no longer valid. People, in the traditional sense of a moral economy, felt they were being cheated. As consumers became aware that trusts—mod-

ern-day engrossers—controlled supplies, operated by collusion, and manipulated prices for immoderate gain, they felt that
their hard-earned money had been extorted from them. Consumers defined prices as being "unreasonable" in a moral, inherent sense, for reasons of want and right. No one had the
right to make excessive profits from the necessities of others.[3]

An advance in the price of few articles would be as keenly
and generally felt as an advance in the cost of meat. The typical
urban consumer, located close to neighborhood stores and
markets, buying supplies in small quantities several times a
week, or perhaps daily, would certainly have been sensitive to
any fluctuations in the price of such a necessity. And while all
classes of consumers would have been affected by periodic price
hikes, the burden certainly fell most heavily on the working
classes. Estimates of the amount of meat (roasting beef, soup
beef, steak, and corned beef) consumed by an average working-class family (five members) varied, but its importance in the
diet of working-class America in the early 20th century was almost universally accepted. One study, completed under the direction of the Board of the University of Chicago Settlement in
1909–1910, showed that the expenditure by working-class families living in the stockyards district of Chicago for foodstuffs
was 53 1/2 percent of all their expenditures. The study noted
that the amounts spent for meat were relatively heavy. Over
four-fifths of all families examined consumed an average of over
one-half pound of meat per day for each adult, and one-quarter
pound of meat per day for every child under age sixteen. The
average working-class family in this section of Chicago was
spending 16 1/2 percent of its total expenditures for meat.[4]

News that the federal government had initiated antitrust
proceedings against the major packing concerns served to intensify the situation in the city. On May 10, 1902, District Attorney S. H. Bethea, acting for U.S. Attorney General Philander C. Knox, filed a bill of complaint against the Beef Trust in
the U.S. Circuit Court in Chicago. Bethea announced that he
would return in ten days to appear before federal judge Peter
S. Grosscup and ask for a temporary injunction against the major meat packers under the Sherman Act. According to Bethea,
the Attorney General's office initiated the action as a result of

communications "from all over the country, volunteering evidence of the illegal practices of the trust."[5] The petition charged the packing companies with conspiracy in restraint of trade and commerce, unlawful combination, blacklisting, illegal cartage charges, and an illegal credit agreement. In addition, the petition alleged the creation of false marketing prices, the illegal depression of the market, and the acceptance of railroad rebates.[6]

Judge Grosscup complied with the wishes of the federal government and granted a temporary injunction against members of the alleged packing combine on May 20, 1902. In support of its case, the government submitted some twenty affidavits that had been collected from individuals previously connected with the packing companies. Daniel W. Meredith, formerly manager for both Armour and Company and Swift and Company, stated that since 1893 the general managers of the "Big Six" packing houses had met on a weekly basis to coordinate operating practices. He charged that the packers set prices, divided marketing territory, and allocated quantities to be sold by the various companies involved. William C. Rider, formerly connected with the Nelson Morris concern, swore that in 1888 he had personally transcribed an agreement between the Morris, Armour, and Swift enterprises. He contended that this agreement set prices, blacklisted discharged employees, and imposed a fine of $1,000 for violations of the compact. Charles E. Holland swore that while employed by the Nelson Morris Company he had transcribed telegrams, received in cipher, that confirmed the existence of such an agreement.[7]

Five days after the Grosscup injunction, the people of Chicago had an opportunity to confront the Beef Trust directly. At midnight on May 25, 1902, 526 teamsters employed at the Union Stockyards to deliver meat to the various distribution houses in Chicago went out on strike. President John Meyers and Business Agent George F. Golden of the Packing House Drivers' Union No. 10 said that the teamsters had tried to get a conference with the packers to present their grievances, but were refused. The strikers were upset over problems of wages and hours. They complained of working from sixteen to eighteen hours a day, without extra pay for overtime, and making from

16 to 25 cents an hour. Their demands included a five to seven cent an hour raise, time and a half for overtime pay, a ten-hour scale, and the right of arbitration in future disputes. If the packers refused to negotiate, the teamsters declared that they would expand the strike to include men that carried meat from the distribution centers to the retail markets, thus raising the threat of a meat famine. To strengthen their case further, the strikers implied that they would be supported by organizations of the Packing Trades Council. Members of the council included nearly every branch of the packing industry in the stockyards. Downtown teamsters, affiliated with the national union and numbering almost 22,000 men, stood as probable supporters as well.[8]

The popular feeling seemed to be that the teamsters had legitimate grounds for complaint. Their wages ranged from a paltry 16 to 25 cents an hour, depending upon the number of horses that they drove.[9] They worked long, irregular, and uncertain hours. The teamsters' occupation was unique because it retained aspects of work that were pre-industrial, aspects of work that were not always compensated for in the industrial system. The teamster had traditionally been required both to care for his stock and drive his wagon. Even when teaming contractors took over the former duties and hired stable men, the driver's role did not substantially change. He still had to report to the barns early and stay late. Wagons constantly needed to be greased and repaired, hitched and unhitched, harnesses needed to be cleaned, and the brass polished. This time-consuming work was classed as "necessary preparation for work," and for this the teamster was usually not paid. The men reported to work well before 6 o'clock in the morning, backed their wagons to the platforms for that first load at 7 o'clock, took one hour for lunch, and tried to get the last load in time to return to the barns by 6 o'clock at night. In the "old days" the driver might not get his last load until the inside workers quit for the day (night), and this could easily keep the teamster busy until after 9 o'clock. The teamster could be called on much earlier in the morning or kept much later at night, according to the amount of work available. As one last injustice, the drivers were forced to give bond in case of lost or stolen meat and required to make good the losses.[10]

On May 27, 1902, the strike in Chicago actively got under-way, and union solidarity actively began to manifest itself. The teamsters resisted attempts by the packers to deliver meat to retailers. Only department superintendents, clerks, and sales-men remained to man company wagons. Strikers surrounded packing-house wagons and forced non-union drivers back to the yards. Union pickets took up positions at the ten entrances to the stockyards, and crowds gathered to make sure that no company wagons attempted to leave. No meat went out, and the beef business in Chicago came to a halt. Eager to move their goods, the packers negotiated with the major express compa-nies, but the drivers of those companies refused to do the work. Some 650 members of the Commission Drivers' Union declined to handle any meat from non-union firms. The packers then appealed to the railroads, but railroad freight-handlers on the Wabash and Erie lines refused to do any work that involved the meat trade. Switchmen on the Belt line would not switch any cars for local consumption. Beef luggers at the Fulton Mar-ket refused to unload wagons that belonged to the major pack-ing companies. Over 200 boxmakers at the National Box Com-pany struck because they had been asked to make boxes for the packers who refused to sign the union agreement. Officers of the union warned all large retail merchants in the city not to accept meat hauled by non-union men. Ice wagon drivers, quick to sympathize with the teamsters, made the warning more em-phatic as they informed butchers that their supplies of ice would be cut off if they continued to deal with non-union drivers. Coal haulers issued their own warning to the suppliers of the large Chicago hotels and major retailers like the Fulton Market with their own ice-making and refrigeration plants. Unless they stopped buying meat from non-union drivers employed by the major packing houses, the supplies of coal that fueled their re-frigeration machines would be cut off. The loss of coal would also endanger what meats they already had on hand. Strikers surrounded the supply houses themselves, determined to pre-vent retail shopkeepers from hauling even a pound of meat away in their own wagons.[11]

By May 31, the situation had become severe. Supplies of meat in butcher shops, meat markets, and restaurants were running short. After five days of the strike, 40 percent of the 1,600 meat markets in the city had exhausted their supplies, 70 percent of the restaurants were forced to scratch meat from their menus, and Chicago's 85,000 Jews were without kosher meat. Soon rumors began to circulate that a general strike, involving 40,000 employees of the stockyards, might be called to assist the teamsters in their fight. The union also notified members in Omaha, Kansas City, St. Joseph, and St. Louis to hold themselves in readiness for a strike against every packing house in the West belonging to the "Big Six." Reportedly, the teamsters' headquarters in Chicago had received assurances from its locals at those points that all the men would obey the summons and go out. President James H. Bowman of the Chicago Federation of Labor also pledged the moral and financial support of his organization to the teamsters' cause. Almost immediately people began to talk of a meat famine.[12]

The packers seemed unperturbed, even in the face of unified labor. Swift and Morris refused even to discuss terms for an agreement and began to import strikebreakers. Men began to arrive in Chicago from Peoria and other towns in the southern part of the state to take the places of the strikers. Rumors circulated that advertisements for workers had been placed in many Illinois newspapers, offering good pay and short hours. The packers objected to the demands of the strikers to employ only members of the Packing House Teamsters' Union, Local No. 10. They did not want to recognize the union formally and be forced to pay union wages. The packers paid only a little over half the union scale and one packer had already calculated on an additional cash outlay of $1,259,000 if he adopted union rates. The packers also objected to a union request for a steward for each barn, appointed by the union, to see that employers faithfully executed all work rules. A *Daily News* reporter aptly recorded the attitude of the packers: "About ten days ago we received a notice that unless we signed an agreement giving the union a right to help run our business there would be a strike. . . . We will shut our doors before we will sign any such agreement."[13] As shortages became acute, beef prices began to climb, and customers once again began to feel the pinch in the cost of a necessary article. Expressions of corporate intransigence and the volatility inherent in price increases had ignited popular sentiments before, but the packers seemed unconcerned.[14]

The contest in Chicago, limited in the beginning to one between the corporation and organized labor, soon broadened into a consumer struggle as well. Utilizing the weapon of the boycott, Chicagoans showed a realization of the crucial link joining their roles as consumers and producers. This added a new dimension to the fight, and undoubtedly surprised the packers with its effectiveness. Chicago newspapers provided daily lists of small slaughtering houses that had signed union-scale contracts so that consumers could have a choice in their meat purchases. These same newspapers also supplied "blacklists" of firms that violated the union picket line. The teamsters' union prepared to circulate updated lists of offenders among the 370 labor unions in the city to discourage patrons from doing business with such traitors. The *Chicago Record Herald* reported that thousands of union men had sworn to uphold the consumer boycott on beef until the packers agreed to terms. The machinists and carpenters joined the boycott by sending orders into the working-class districts that all consumers should refrain from making purchases from the major meat companies.[15]

Support for the boycott also began to surface from the more than 1,200 butchers in the city as shops began to close in support of the strikers. The *Chicago Evening Post* reported: "Practically all the retail butchers are with the strikers and buy stock from the packers who have signed the union scale."[16] In the district southwest of the stockyards, over 200 small butchers closed their doors. In the Jewish ghetto, kosher meat merchants, shut off from their slaughtering house in the Armour plant, notified the strikers that they had formed an agreement not to buy meat until the strike ended. In south Chicago a group of twenty Polish butchers went to the strike committee and said that they would not open their stores until they could get meat from companies that had signed the union scale. The Bohemian Butchers' Association, composed of several hundred retail dealers, also agreed to the meat boycott in support of the strikers. Two hundred butchers on the northwest side of Chicago followed suit. The Retail Butchers' Association also issued an appeal to the 400 women near the stockyards who patronized the retail markets of Armour and Company to withdraw their trade.[17]

At least one butcher saw his participation in the strike as being more than support for exploited workers. The strike and boycott also held out hope to him for the opportunity to throw off trust dominance and regain a feeling of independence and control over his life as a small businessman. As he stated: "We [butchers] are still doing business at the old stands under direction of the packers. They tell us the price and we must pay it. The word 'butcher' as applied to the retail handler of meats has long since become a misnomer. The packers are the butchers in all that the word implies. We are the victims of the butchers."[18] Butchers had lost their traditional role as independent craftsmen in the preparation of meat. The packers, with their assembly-line methods, had acquired the economic power to dictate to the small retailer. The right of the union to exist served as a rallying point around which workers, butchers, and consumers could express their displeasure. Workers complained of trust control over their trade. Butchers complained of the prices they had to pay for meat, and that they had no choice but to pass the charges on to their customers. Consumers complained of trust control over the prices of a necessary item. Chicagoans, provided with a common enemy, seemed to be rediscovering the age-old sense of community.

Consumers, concerned for the legitimate plight of workers exploited by the corporation, also began to define a consciousness of their own. This related directly to the current economic situation as well as to the cultural backgrounds of many consumers. Simon Mayor, a merchant, remarked that there were "going to be closed-up shops and men hungry for meat if this [strike] keeps on. There will be many meatless dinners on Sunday, but I have yet to see a patron who is not in sympathy with the men."[19] Stanislaus Lewandowski, a shopkeeper, observed that since the increase in the price of meats, customers had been purchasing more groceries. As the price of meat climbed, consumers switched to fish, canned goods, cheese, fruits, and other staple articles. In fact, consumption of those items doubled. The poultry business also increased 100 percent during the first week of the strike. High meat prices and the difficulty of getting meat definitely affected meat trade. Many consumers, either driven by price or motivated by the boycott, quickly expressed their defiance of the trust and altered their diets. But for many immigrant groups the choice might not have been so easily made. For Poles, Jews, Lithuanians, and other ethnic groups the consumption of meat and even certain types of meat was part of their cultural heritage. The high rates of meat consumption mentioned earlier suggests that this was indeed true. To a Polish family, for instance, the removal of pork from the family diet could well have violated tradition and further degraded the family's status in the community. It could also have been one additional factor working to build popular anger and a willingness to confront directly the antagonist, the Beef Trust.[20]

The strike also provided an opportunity for Chicagoans to release pent-up emotions that had been generated by the exactions of a trust, the symbol of corporate modernization. On May 30, the *Chicago Daily News* reported that holiday crowds blocked wagons driven by strikebreakers and cheered the strikers. Playing dirges, hymns, and funeral marches, a band hired by the striking teamsters located itself in front of Swift and Company's store in the Fulton Market. A large crowd of strike sympathizers shouted approval of each new tune suggestive of the packer's predicament. Such tunes included "Nearer My God To Thee," and "Massa's in de Cold, Cold Ground." However, this lighter mood did not last long, especially after the major newspapers carried an open letter to Mayor Carter Harrison from the Chicago Federation of Labor. The letter charged that the packers' combine had unlawfully conspired against the public. To substantiate their accusations, the Federation reminded readers that for years those same packing houses had tapped the city's water mains and had stolen the city's water. They had continued to evade the equitable assessment of their property, immunity for which the practice of bribery could be the only acceptable explanation. They had also sold rotten and worthless meat during the Spanish-American War, killing more men with this "canned" and "embalmed" meat than the entire Spanish Army. And, according to evidence made known to the public through the antitrust proceedings of recent weeks, they had engaged in a criminal conspiracy against 78,000,000 people.[21]

The day the Federation's accusations appeared, riots broke out in the city of Chicago and continued for the next several days. Starting in the working-class districts bordering on the Chicago River and in the northwest portion of the city, teamsters of coal and iron wagons blocked the packing-house delivery wagons and streets became impassable. Drivers left their wagons amid great cheering from crowds that numbered into the thousands, and joined the mass of "roaring and howling humanity." When a coal teamster blocked the path of a Swift and Company wagon, the police attempted to arrest him. The crowd, however, tore the man from the arresting authorities and surrounded his abandoned wagon and team. When the packers attempted to send a train of thirty-five wagon loads of meat into the downtown area with a police escort, men stalked the wagons from their starting point and jeered the scab drivers as they progressed. At the corner of Clark and Harrison Streets the crowds had increased to several thousands, and fifty policemen were forced to use clubs to prevent the wagons from being overturned. At Halstead and Division Streets, police engaged in a hand-to-hand struggle with several thousand strike sympathizers. At State and Adams the crowds had increased to "fully 50,000" and 100 policemen responded to clear a path for wagons to be driven back to the yards. Crowds forced police to send in fire alarms to clear the steets. The heavy fire trucks responding to the calls raced through the streets and scattered the crowds. On the Lake Street bridge, a crowd engulfed a nonunion meat driver and forced him to abandon his wagon. Quickly, a union driver took his place. The man then stuck a union card in his hat and drove away, the "crowd melting before him like magic." Such pro-labor support also expressed itself on Fifth Avenue where three men, employed by a hat manufacturer, moved onto a fire-escape and threw "missile after missile" into the street. One of the men commented: "We are union men and have no sympathy for these [non-union] fellows."[22] Striking linemen, in sympathy with the teamsters, cut all the wires to the North Side order departments and distribution depots of the packers. At Halstead, Root, State, and Forty-Second Streets and on Wabash Avenue crowds gathered at every intersection and hurled "derisive epithets" at the passing drivers. At Van Buren and State a caravan of meat wagons encountered a volley of decayed fruit and eggs. At Monroe and State twenty wagons blocked the way as throngs of people congested and controlled the streets in the central district of the city.[23]

Although the riot exhibited a strong working-class bias from the beginning, other aspects of the crowd's behavior revealed deeper layers of involvement. When the street activity became hectic, it seemed as though the entire community became involved. As the crowds increased in numbers, they changed in character as well. Class distinctions and established sex roles blurred in the process, and elements of the middle class appeared to lend their support to the strike. "Arm to arm with teamsters wearing dirty clothes and greasy aprons were young women in summer gowns and well-dressed clerks and businessmen."[24] Several women could be seen in the street pushing their way through the crowds to get beside the wagons of the blockading teamsters. Carrying baskets of carnations, they tossed these upon the heroes. Women in the windows along the street let out a "feminine cheer" and waved handkerchiefs in support. Streetcar traffic became snarled as the streets became congested. But the predominantly women passengers seemed to accept the delay. During a blockade of meat wagons, a number of "well-dressed women" on a Division Street car cheered the crowd's attempt to prevent the delivery of meat. One woman in particular, said to be the wife of a well-known real estate man, was nicknamed the "Teamsters' Joan of Arc" for her enthusiasm in the strike. Leaning out of the windows of buildings along the adjoining blocks, men, women, and boys cheered the teamsters and their supporters. "The waiting sympathizers of the striking teamsters seemed to spring from the ground."[25] Down in the street sympathizers threw eggs, bottles, and spools of thread at policemen and scabs, with many women taking a most active part in the riot. According to the chief of police: "The women are the most dangerous persons with whom the police have to deal. They gather at the windows along the line of march and throw anything at the drivers or patrolmen."[26] When one of the meat wagons stopped at White's Market to make a delivery, women and men employed in the wholesale stores in the vicinity threw pieces of nailed plank, bottles, and remnants of their lunches. When arrested, some women pleaded so hard for release that they were freed, only to rejoin the crowd and resume their "jeering" and "cat-calls."[27]

Crowd composition and participation revealed that such riot-ous activity had become a community action. Pro-labor sym-pathy, consumer hardship, and citizen outrage obscured class distinctions. Many women undoubtedly participated in the riots as working-class wives and neighbors. But women also pur-chased the food and administered the family budget. They were the ones who had control over meals and diet, and had found that they could no longer consume in the old manner. Being involved with everyday marketing, women were more sensi-tive to price fluctuations. They were also most experienced in detecting short-weights and items of inferior quality. They readily understood the consumer point of view. Chicagoans cooper-ated against the anti-union activities of the major meat-packing companies, but they also chose to attack the modern-day "en-grosser." No one had an absolute right to monopolize vital commodities or to control the necessities of life. The exactions of the Beef Trust forced people to realize that the industrial cor-poration had established control over production and con-sumption. Crowd activity offered them a means to vent all of these frustrations.[28]

In choosing to stand between striking workers and strike sympathizers on one hand and the packing-house corporations and strikebreakers on the other, the police became associated with the latter. As a result, police participation in the strike provided an additional provocation to those engaged in street activities. The Chicago police department decided almost from the beginning to protect property and maintain order in the city. Mayor Harrison stood firmly behind the police and stated: "The streets are free to everyone, citizens or not. There is nothing more demoralizing than street disturbances because they teach contempt for the law. It is the paramount duty of the police to stop them. The police department is neutral and is to be used to suppress disorder."[29] At the first signs of popular resistance to the transportation of meat through the city, the police began to escort caravans of wagons to their downtown distribution points. The Chicago Federation of Labor objected that this police "neutrality" really amounted to outright police protection for the packers, corporations accused of unlawfully conspiring against the public good. When the police began to protect this "lawless" element, they became lawbreakers instead of law enforcers from the viewpoint of many Chicagoans. When 200 policemen rode out with a meat caravan, strike sympathizers blockaded the convoy at sixteen different points along the way. The unruly crowd forced the procession to make an exhaustive nine-hour trip to the supply depots and back to the yards.[30]

The police had become the "tools" of the packers, and the protected caravans had the look of defying the public interest. What followed appeared almost as a natural result of the circumstances and appearances that had been created. When the police attempted to make arrests, crowds responded by attacking them to free those who had been apprehended. One woman by the name of Lizzie Malloy, arrested by the police for throwing a brick during a street disturbance, defended her action by stating: "Men, I just had to do it."[31] The editor of the *Journal*, intrigued as much by the statement as the act itself, attempted an explanation for his readers.

That impulse of just having to do it was latent in the hearts of thousands who watched the procession of police and wagons. . . .

The fat officers, the coatless drivers and the red wagons had taken on new aspects that fairly invited a man [or woman] to come out and be violent.

Legal and proper as the whole process was, it had the look of a spectacular defiance.[32]

Police continued to club interfering demonstrators, and crowds in the streets and individuals from buildings along the lines of march threw bricks, stones, sticks, and lumps of coal in response. The crowds cursed and jeered the police and the strikebreaking drivers together. Policemen and scabs also served as the indiscriminate targets of objects. Both had become allies of the Beef Trust in the public mind. The alleged trust had been charged with fixing prices and restraining trade, with stealing the city's water and selling embalmed beef, and with dodging equitable tax assessments and arrogantly refusing arbitration. From such a perspective, crowd activity gained a rationale of its own. Rioting and lawlessness served as justifiable actions, because the police had failed to protect the welfare of the community, and had chosen instead to support "tyrannical" corporations. The crowds, in turn, assumed the role that had been abandoned by law enforcement officials, and began to act as defenders of the public welfare. The crowd had established its own sense of legitimacy.[33]

The strike finally ended on June 5, 1902. The strike had lasted nearly two weeks, the last three days of which major rioting occurred and thousands of people became involved. Frederick W. Job of the State Board of Arbitration assisted union leaders and packing-house representatives in finally reaching a settlement. Under the new pact the teamsters agreed to return to work on a compromise basis. The union waived the demand for formal recognition of their union and shop steward in return for tacit recognition. The packers, in turn, promised that further disagreements would be settled by arbitration and agreed to a wage increase. New pay rates moved upward and ranged from 18 to 30 cents per hour or from $12.60 to $21.00 per seventy-hour work week. Before the strike some workers had earned as little as $13.50 for a week of 120 hours. The packers still refused to employ only union men, but pledged not to discriminate against those carrying union cards.[34]

Popular indignation towards trusts and combinations of all types burst into the open in Chicago in May and June of 1902, and focused on the Beef Trust. A labor dispute over wages, hours, union recognition, and a degree of control over the means of production quickly merged with consumer complaints over corporate control of one of life's necessities. Small businessmen, chafing under corporate dominance in the marketplace, joined in support of a massive consumer boycott. The expanded result was an event that had increased in complexity. The community became involved, and the discontented poured out into the streets. Participation in the ensuing street riot transcended sex and class distinctions as the crowds swelled in numbers and sent their own message of dissatisfaction to the trust. Police involvement took on the appearance of support for corporate malfeasance, and violence became a justifiable action. In the process, the people of Chicago demonstrated their awareness of the control that the beef monopoly had over their lives and they resisted. For the riot to be effective, it did not require a great deal of organization, but it did require the collective support of the community.

The Chicago teamsters' strike, and the riot in which it culminated, should be seen as an expression of changing popular attitudes toward monopoly. The historical significance of the strike and riot does not reside solely in the event as an example of working-class consciousness. Chicagoans, as workers, consumers, taxpayers, and citizens took to the streets to resist the implications of corporate modernization. Industrial expansion and corporate mergers and consolidations affected the thoughts and actions of the people influenced by them. The dispute between the teamsters and the packers and the street riots, boycotts, and crowd activities in general, provided examples of actions indicative of these changes. Even the *Chicago Socialist*, ideologically tuned to look for the class-conscious nuances involved in such strikes, editorially admitted that something "new" had taken place:

It is not strange that the tremendous economic changes which have taken place in the past few years should produce a corresponding change in the modes of thought and action of the people influenced by them.

Even the recent street riots, incident upon the dispute between the packers and teamsters, showed some peculiar features, probably indicative of this change.

A personal contact with the crowds participating in them showed conclusively that it was by no means the so-called "tough elements," the "hoodlums" that preponderated. It . . . is certainly undeniable that most of the sympathizers who took an active part in the disturbances were well dressed people, many of whom from their appearance belonged to the little middle class.

A canvas of the small store keepers undertaken by some of our party members, showed that this class was almost unanimous in favor of

the strikers. In previous strikes this element was always the most bitterly opposed to the workingmen and never failed to display its hostility.[35]

The response differed because the nature of the event had
changed. Workers had lost control over their workplace and with
that the security of being able to provide for a family. Small retailers had relinquished control over inventories and prices, and,
once again, one's security had been assumed by others. Consumers found that impersonal forces controlled product quality, safety, selection, and price. There seemed to be no avenue
of redress for complaint, no one to assume ultimate responsibility.

The Chicago strike, in a participatory sense, was part of the
nationwide antitrust movement that had been building since the
late 1890s. Though no immediate legislative or judicial benefits
resulted directly from the event, it did contribute to the larger
antitrust movement. State and national policymakers did react
to a groundswell of popular sentiment and intensify the enactment, revision, and enforcement of antitrust statutes. In new
ways, the participants at Chicago reasserted their claim to ultimate responsibility. They reaffirmed their commitment to a
moral, inherent ideology of proper economic action and social
obligation.

THE FIGHT AGAINST STANDARD OIL

6

During the first decade of the 20th century, with the antitrust movement in full force, popular attention focused on the Standard Oil Company. The Standard typified the greatest of all industrial combinations—its control of transportation, refining, and marketing mechanisms was well known to those in the industry, and newspaper articles and muckraking exposés explained the details of such control to the general public. But people also learned about Standard Oil as they had learned about other trusts and monopolies. Control of an industry by one concern, or by a combination of concerns, meant higher freight charges to competitors, lower raw material prices to producers, higher prices to consumers for the finished products, bribed politicians, and higher taxes.[1] But it meant more than that. When a trust gained control over an area, it either absorbed or eliminated independent operators. In each case their economic independence disappeared. Late 19th century industrialization and economic consolidation occurred at such a rapid pace that people could feel the control over their lives being jerked from them. And not everyone accepted either the economic process which seemed to deify bigness or the implications of subservience. Many people chose to resist in their roles as independent producers, as consumers, or as citizens of their local community, state, or nation. They organized, boycotted, and pressured their legal and political representatives. These common bonds of popular resistance forced states to employ the legal device of antitrust to attack the Standard Oil Company, while, at the same time, they compelled the federal government to challenge the Standard over antitrust and railroad rate violations.

Two developments characterized the early history of the Standard Oil Company: a drive on the part of the corporation to establish centralization of authority and systematization and secrecy in the operation of its interests, and, at the same time, a hostile reaction on the part of the public to the means and implications of that process. The trust concept had been utilized by Standard Oil men as early as 1879, but only as a temporary device for holding the securities of a group of investors and not as an instrument of managerial control. Formalization of the Standard Oil Trust Agreement took place on January 2, 1882. The agreement set up a trust, or central holding arrangement, which included forty specifically named companies. Forty-one stockholders engaged in all aspects of petroleum operations—buying, transporting, storing, refining, and marketing—signed the agreement and exchanged their properties for Trust certificates, which, as a total, were valued at $70,000,000. Control centered in nine trustees who were to supervise the business operations of the Standard Oil Companies and any other companies or partnerships belonging to the Trust. The agreement provided for the establishment of corporations, bearing the Standard Oil name, in New Jersey, Ohio, New York, and Pennsylvania, and left power to the trustees to organize similar corporations in other states.[2]

The Standard's operations also placed it prominently in a hostile public eye as the symbol of bigness, a creature of the railroad rebate, and an enemy of free enterprise capitalism. During the 1870s, newspaper accounts enabled the public to connect John D. Rockefeller and his associates with the South Improvement Company, which the public saw as a scheme, undertaken in cooperation with the railroads, to force independent refiners in the Ohio region into the Standard association. In 1881, Henry Demarest Lloyd increased national exposure of Standard Oil methods by publishing an article, "The Story of a Great Monopoly," in the March issue of the *Atlantic Monthly*. Lloyd's primary attack centered on the railroads, but he cited the Standard Oil Company as an example of a monopoly established as a consequence of privileges gained from the railroads. Preferential treatment in the form of rebates accounted for

Standard Oil's monopolistic power which included ownership of pipe lines, control of refining, and dominance in the marketing of products such as kerosene. Lloyd informed his readers that the Standard used this power to destroy competitors.[3]

Not only independent producers but the broader community of consumers and taxpayers also felt the presence of Standard Oil's power. In the late 1880s, Toledo, Ohio, was the scene of one such contest between the people and the Standard Oil Company over the problem of supplying that city with natural gas. As the debate heated, the issue quickly became one of municipally owned versus privately owned supplies of natural gas. But the events in Toledo were significant in showing the actions and attitudes of the people in regard to the Standard Oil Company, even in that early period. The proponents of municipal ownership often spoke of the "extent and power of the gigantic monopoly [Standard Oil]," and of the dangers of entering into competition with such a powerful concern. Those promoting the sale of municipal bonds to establish municipal ownership in Toledo successfully used as their slogan "The city against the Standard Oil," and convinced citizens and taxpayers of the need to protect their community from the "aggressions of colossal power."[4]

Though the people in the oil regions of Ohio and Pennsylvania had been experiencing, at close hand, the exactions of the Standard Oil Company for years, other Americans received their lesson in trust economics from the muckrakers. During the depression of the 1890s, Henry Demarest Lloyd expanded his earlier study of Standard Oil into book form with his popular account entitled *Wealth Against Commonwealth*. Lloyd's prophetic description of the people under the thumb of monopoly preceded the detailed account of Ida M. Tarbell, but was no more influential in focusing public attention and in developing the sinister image of the Standard Oil Company. Tarbell combined the journalism of exposure with the popular appeal of the muckraking journals to reach a vast readership. Beginning in 1902, and continuing for two years thereafter, Tarbell published her *History of the Standard Oil Company* in serial form in *McClure's* and drew unprecedented popular attention to the methods of the Standard Oil Trust.

The efforts of journalists to inform the public did not go

without reward, as several early investigations were undertaken to curb the power of the Standard. Attorney General David K. Watson of Ohio made the first successful attack on the Standard when he initiated a common law suit in May of 1890 to revoke the charter of the Standard Oil Company of Ohio. He based his suit upon allegations that the Standard Oil Company [Ohio] had extended beyond its charters and had merged into another corporation—the Standard Oil Trust. In March, 1892, the Ohio Supreme Court upheld the information of the attorney general and prohibited the Ohio Standard from remaining as a part of the trust agreement. When the State of Ohio revoked its charter, the trust fled to New Jersey and incorporated under the laws there. In November, 1897, Frank S. Monnett, Attorney General of Ohio, again instituted action against the Standard Oil Company by filing information of contempt against the Ohio branch of the corporation for failing to divorce itself from the trust. Monnett went on to initiate *quo warranto* proceedings against several Standard Oil properties in Ohio, and demanded forfeiture of charters in violation of the state's recently enacted anti-trust law. Though the attempts in Ohio proved unsuccessful in court, Texas officials concluded a successful suit in 1900 against the Waters-Pierce Oil Company—a Standard subsidiary—for having engaged in unfair marketing practices in violation of that state's antitrust law. But these investigative actions at the state level gained little assistance from the federal government. A Congressional Committee on Manufactures conducted an investigation of the oil industry in 1888, and the Industrial Commission, an agency of the federal government, initiated another investigation of trusts in 1899. The findings of this second commission resulted in the creation of the Department of Commerce and the Bureau of Corporations, but, once again, no direct action. And this was how things stood until the people of Kansas decided to do battle with the "Octopus" in the winter of 1904–1905.[5]

Oil formed a part of people's lives in Kansas even before the Civil War. Accounts show that farmers near the old Santa Fe Trail probably skimmed off oil from tar springs and sold it to travelers or teamsters for lubricating purposes. Until the 1890s, oil exploration in Kansas remained an adventure, characterized by sporadic "Wildcatting" operations. Then, in 1892, William M. Mills, a Pennsylvania operator who had gone broke in that state during the 1880s, discovered the first large quantity of crude oil near Neodesha, Kansas. Mills soon sold his interests to the Guffy and Gailey Company, which had extensive oil-producing operations in Pennsylvania. In 1895 Guffy and Gailey sold out to the Forest Oil Company, a subsidiary of the Standard Oil Company. In effect, the Standard both anticipated and created a market for oil in Kansas by establishing a refinery at Neodesha in 1897 that could process 500 barrels of oil a day. The refined oil would be shipped in tank cars from there to Kansas City. In 1899, with oil selling at 75 cents per barrel at Neodesha, another Standard concern, the Kansas Oil and Gas Company, absorbed the Forest Oil Company. By 1901 the name had been changed to the Prairie Oil and Gas Company, oil was selling at 80 cents a barrel, and Kansans started to catch "oil fever." Oil and gas were discovered near Chanute, Kansas, in Neosho County. Success bred success, and the Prairie Oil and Gas Company laid pipe lines from Chanute to Neodesha and bought the oil. Discoveries then followed in Chautauqua County, the town of Peru became an oil center, and oil began selling at $1.10 a barrel. The Kansas oil rush was underway.[6]

Everybody, it seemed, had gone oil crazy. Oil wells began to appear in nearly every back yard, church yard, and even in some cemeteries in the boom towns of the oil regions. Soon oil companies appeared in almost every city in the state. One reporter estimated that seven out of every ten people he met in the streets or on the train traveling through Kansas were stockholders in some company. A pool of $10,000 would be enough to send a representative into the oil region to buy a lease. Leases would give an eighth or a tenth to the farmer or speculator who owned the land. Promoters advertised in regional papers and scores of producers who had been "busted" in the Ohio and Pennsylvania fields, where the Standard already had destroyed competition, filtered into Kansas. Estimates circulated that from 500 to 600 companies were doing business in Kansas and working the oil regions.[7]

But beneath the oil mania there was perhaps a deeper force motivating many Kansans, Ohioans, and Pennsylvanians in the oil fields—the quest for economic independence. Kansas farmers had complained loudly during the 1880s and 1890s of exorbitant railroad rates, burdensome interest charges, depressed prices on farm crops or stock, and oppressive prices for farm implements, for binding twine, or for the staple products, finished goods or fuel they purchased as consumers. In the words of one sympathetic writer, farmers were being "robbed by an infamous system of finance . . . plundered by transportation companies . . . deprived of their lands and other property by an iniquitous system of usury . . . fleeced by the exorbitant exactions of numerous trusts . . . [and] preyed upon by the merchants."[8] And Kansans knew who to blame for these economic injustices. Experience had introduced them to the railroad monopoly, the money trust, the binding twine trust, the beef trust, the plow trust, and the tin, lumber, or milling trusts. Kansans felt as if their old ways of life, ways in which they thought they had control over the things they produced and the things they consumed, were being taken from them. During the late 1880s the people of Kansas had sought to regain that control by joining the cooperatives and exchanges of the Farmers' Alliance. With the "oil rush," like the gold rushes before, the opportunity to strike-it-rich presented them with the possibility of regaining the economic independence they had lost.[9] Many of the producers from Ohio and Pennsylvania were no different. They had not rejected the capitalist system, but had, instead, been unfairly rejected by it. As independent producers they had been cheated and tricked by forces of collusion over which they had no control. And just as the Kansas farmer placed the blame on the emerging concentrations of economic power, so too did the eastern oil producers. Experience had taught them that the railroads, in league with the greatest of all trusts, Standard Oil, had taken from them the economic freedom to which they aspired.[10]

With the price of oil at \$1.10 in 1903, the economic outlook loomed bright and production increased. But for all this oil there was only one purchaser—the Standard. As investment in Kansas increased, the Standard Oil Company extended its operations for handling the output. Price increases further stimulated production, and the Standard expanded its refining at

Neodesha to process 3,000 barrels of oil a day. Still production increased and the Standard built a 10,000 barrel refinery at Sugar Creek, Missouri, just outside Kansas City. The Standard completed the refinery in September, 1904, and a pipe line connected it with the oil field and storage tank farms at Neodesha, Humboldt, and Caney, Kansas. Production continued to exceed refining capacity, and the Standard began to extend its pipe line eastward to Whiting, Indiana, the central refining depot of the Standard Oil Company. Then the prosperous climate in Kansas began to change. The Prairie Oil and Gas Company began to purchase oil by a specific gravity test, which eliminated some Kansas oil from the market and reduced the price on top-grade oil. From a peak of $1.38 in late 1903 it dropped to 70 cents in six months. Finally, in the late summer of 1904, just as the pipe line to Sugar Creek was nearing completion, the freight rates on oil shipped in tank cars increased from 10 cents to 17 cents a hundred pounds. Kansas producers could no longer afford to ship oil out of the state and were forced to sell to the Prairie Oil and Gas Company, that then shipped through its pipe line to Sugar Creek. But when the price of refined oil refused to drop along with the price of crude oil, many people began to wonder about profits. They knew that buyers purchased oil for 70 cents a barrel (42 gallons for crude), but they also knew that wholesalers sold the refined product for $3.60 a barrel (30 gallons for refined), a significant discrepancy. The Standard had only one independent rival, the Webster refinery at Humboldt. When Webster sold oil at Emporia or other towns below the Standard price, the trust cut its figure by a cent a gallon, but merchants continued to buy oil from the independent. These developments came to a climax in Kansas in the winter of 1904–1905. Profits diminished and investors became angry. But beneath the anger was fear. Discrimination in freight rates and the absence of competition had made the Standard and its pipe lines controlling factors in the situation. And once again the people of Kansas experienced the feeling of being economically dependent.[11]

At the end of July, 1904, popular indignation in Kansas began to coalesce and to directly affect politics in the state. Kansans held mass meetings in the oil districts. Oil was the theme of almost every gathering, even among women's clubs. People were upset as investors and producers. The *Topeka Capital* estimated that 31,000 Kansans had invested in oil, of which 20,000 were stockholders, 5,000 were individual operators, and 6,000 were landowners who had granted lease rights. But the people were also upset as consumers, as retail buyers of kerosene and refined oil, and they reacted to what they regarded as price imposition on the part of the Standard. Oil and gasoline stoves replaced those of coal and wood, while automobiles and gasoline-operated machinery increased the demand for the refined product. Kansas, which produced its own crude oil, also paid more for refined oil than many other states did even though the refined oil was shipped from greater distances. In November, S. M. Porter, an oil producer, was elected to the Kansas Senate, and conceived of the idea of a state-owned oil refinery. In explaining his objectives Porter stated that his plan was designed "to create legislative competition and then other competition would follow. I wanted to encourage independent refineries in the State so that all the oil would not have to go to one corporation."[12] When the press publicized Porter's idea, many attacked it as being socialistic. The editor of the *Ottawa Herald* politely acknowledged his reservations about the plan, but was also cognizant of the sentiment working in favor of its passage. He concluded that the "undoubted preponderance of public opinion for the refinery" made a significant statement in reference to the trust question. The people favored the idea because it promised to strike a blow at the Standard Oil Trust. The editor noted that there "are even to be found in every community men of careful business judgement who are willing to waive prejudices against state interference in private business . . . for the sake of curbing the power of Standard Oil."[13] Porter found support from newly elected Republican Governor E. W. Hoch who stated in his message to the Kansas legislature on January 9, 1905, that he was inclined to put aside his objections to the socialistic aspects of the Porter proposal. As the governor lamented, "we are being ground between the upper and nether millstones of monopoly, and the people are rightfully demanding relief."[14] A state-owned refinery seemed to offer a means of protection for producers who struggled to sell their crude oil and for consumers forced to pay too much for the final product.[15]

While talk of a state refinery bill circulated, oil producers in Kansas sought their own form of organization. Led by H. E. West, an oil producer at Peru, Kansas oil men formed the Kansas Oil Producer's Association. Two hundred oil producers met at the Throop Hotel in Topeka on January 19, 1905, and adopted a set of resolutions declaring for a state refinery, a common carrier pipe line bill, an anti-discrimination bill, and a maximum railroad rate bill. The Association then began a campaign to gain popular support for their measures once they had been introduced in the state legislature. They published a short leaflet entitled "That the People May Know," and printed newspaper extracts in support of their position as well as anti-Rockefeller cartoons. The Association placed a "tax" of 50 cents on every well of its members to defray the costs of publication, and sent a different circular out every day. They also obtained a list of every township trustee in the state and the name of every farmer on file with the State Department of Agriculture, and mailed to each a letter that described the efforts of the Standard to control the consumer and independent producer of oil. Citizens across the state responded by returning letters, telegrams, and petitions to the state legislature urging the passage of the pro-Association oil measures. A Western Kansas anti-horse-thief association even offered its services. Others were angry enough to take to the stump to vent their emotions. T. B. Murdock, said to be close to the state administration, excited a crowd in Topeka with threats directed at the Standard:

After a little the people of the country will raise up and hang a few Rockefellers and other kinds of buzzards who rob the people, not forgetting to include in the general hangings a squad or two of high court judges. . . .

Everything we eat, everything we drink, is either controlled by a trust or is adulterated. Congress will do nothing, so it is time for the people to begin to get ready to do something.[16]

Murdock also received a warm response to his suggestion that Standard Oil lobbyists should be tarred and feathered.[17]

In an effort to appease consumers, the Standard, on February 10, reduced the retail price of kerosene. But consumers regarded the cut as an admission that prices had been kept too high. Then, to intimidate producers, the Standard issued orders that no more Kansas oil would be purchased by the Prairie Oil and Gas Company, and stated that all construction work in the field would be stopped. This boycott by the Standard served to intensify support for the Association and assured passage of the pending legislation. One producer, who had everything tied up in his oil investment, stated that he would willingly let his wells stay plugged up for ten years rather than let the Standard win out. House Speaker W. R. Stubbs thought it "a very silly way to try to influence a legislature and especially a legislature made up of Kansas men."[18] And even a prominent Standard official in Independence, Kansas, admitted that the company had never "put its foot in it" so seriously.[19]

The agitation in Kansas resulted in a legislative assault on all fronts. The refinery bill passed, as did the bill fixing maximum freight rates on railroads for the transportation of oil in tank cars or barrels. The legislature also enacted the anti-discrimination bill which prohibited any person or corporation from selling a commodity cheaper in one part of the state than in another. The pipe line carrier bill completed the legislative package by making every pipe line in the state a common carrier, like the railroads, and placed them under the authority of the State Board of Railway Commissioners. The owners of the pipe line had to furnish storage tanks where they obtained the crude oil, and grant a certificate of quantity and quality at that time. The crude oil would then have to be forwarded in order of its receipt. Upon passage of these measures the Atchison, Topeka, and Santa Fe Railroad announced rates in Kansas conforming to the maximum freight rate bill.[20]

Probably even more startling to Standard Oil officials was the notification that legislative action was being instituted at the federal level as well. On February 14, 1905, Representative Philip Campbell of Kansas introduced a resolution in the House of Representatives requesting the secretary of commerce to investigate the causes of the low price of crude oil in the Kansas field and the unusually large margin between the price of crude oil and the selling price of refined oil and its by-products. On February 15, the House unanimously adopted the resolution. In response to the action of Congress, President Theodore Roosevelt directed James R. Garfield, the commissioner of corporations, to begin an immediate oil investigation.[21] As complaints had also been received from other new oil fields in Texas and California, Garfield broadened the investigation to encompass the entire oil industry.[22]

Events in Kansas sparked activity in other states as well. In Muncie, Indiana, independent oil operators from the various Indiana fields claimed the Standard was discriminating in marketing and in pipe line rates and attempting to "freeze out" the independent producer. They urged the legislature to pass the antitrust law currently before it. State Representative Clifton Hilder introduced a state refinery bill in the Colorado legislature, while the Texas legislature had bills pending to establish a state refinery and to make pipe lines common carriers. Iowa telegraphed the Kansas legislature for copies of the new oil laws, and Oklahoma considered the possibility of erecting a state refinery and gave notice that a bill compelling corporations to maintain uniform prices throughout the state would be introduced. In the Illinois legislature a resolution was introduced that called for the appointment of a committee to discuss the extent of Standard Oil pipe lines with the Kansas legislature. The Illinois House also adopted a resolution offering to loan the State of Kansas $100,000, without interest for a period of six years, to aid in the construction of the state's oil refinery. Missouri also chose to jump into the fight, and bills declaring pipe lines common carriers and fixing a maximum rate of freight were introduced in Jefferson City. On February 12, 1905, Standard Oil stock sold for $600 a share, a decline of 31 points over a seven-day period, the result of agitation against the company by the President, Congress, and the states.[23]

The oil fight in Kansas did not subside with the passage of the anti-Standard legislation, but it soon became apparent that other states would have to assist Kansas if lasting economic freedom were ever to be achieved. Legislative successes prompted independent oil companies in Kansas to make elaborate plans for pipe lines and refineries. On March 18, 1905, 3,000 persons took part in an oil producer's convention in Independence, Kansas with Ida M. Tarbell as one of the guest speakers. The purpose of the convention was to continue the popular campaign against the Standard. On July 4, Kansas signaled its independence day by opening its first anti-Standard plant, known as the Uncle Sam Refinery. Kansans were probably more excited than ever in their celebration of ultimate triumph over Standard Oil. But this mood was not to last. On July 7, the Kansas State Supreme Court declared the independent refinery bill unconstitutional, and many producers saw that there would be continued problems with railroad rate charges as well. The maximum freight rate and anti-discrimination laws passed in Kansas enabled producers to ship their freight at low rates inside the state, but exorbitant rates awaited them at their state borders. The examples were endless. The shipping rate from Chanute, Kansas, to Kansas City, Kansas—125 miles—was 7 1/2 cents per hundred pounds. But the rate from Chanute, Kansas, to Kansas City, Missouri—127 miles—was 17 cents. Oil shipped from Chanute to Weber, Kansas—254 miles—was 10 1/2 cents, but to ship it seven miles farther on the same road, to Superior, Nebraska, was 30 cents. Without the assistance of other states, Kansas producers could not broaden their selling market.[24]

In the face of such a predicament the Kansas Oil Producer's Association decided on a vigorous offensive campaign throughout the country for what it considered to be "equitable" and "just" freight rates on crude and refined oils. Independent producers and refiners in Kansas claimed to have information to prove the existence of rate discrimination and market control by the railroads and the Standard Oil Company. Letters were sent to governors of states with winter legislative sessions urging them to pass legislation similar to the Kansas laws. The Association planned to furnish each legislator with a copy of a report setting forth the advantages of such enactments. They also planned to send a memorial to President Roosevelt and a petition to Commissioner Garfield urging them to support measures for oil relief in the West. The Association also made plans for a special subcommittee to visit all state capitals, and had been in correspondence with Governors Robert La Follette (Wisconsin), Joseph Folk (Missouri), Charles Deneen (Illinois), and Albert Cummins (Iowa) urging their support.[25]

The emotions of the people seemed just as resilient as those of the Kansas Oil Producer's Association. The town of Iola, Kansas, planned to conduct an experiment with crude oil on its streets. The Standard offered to donate the oil to the city, but the city council declined the offer and purchased the oil from an independent. All the grocers in the town signed a pledge that they would not patronize the Standard Oil Company as long as they could get independent oil. In some towns none of the people would buy groceries from a man who patronized the Standard.[26]

Anti-Standard activity continued in states other than Kansas. Various state attorneys general, of whom Herbert Hadley of Missouri figured most prominently, became increasingly alert to Standard Oil methods. The Missouri legislature was about to pass its own maximum freight rate bill when Hadley first became involved with the Standard Oil Company. While participating in hearings before the State Board of Railway Commissioners on complaints brought by independent oil dealers in Missouri, he made inquiries concerning the trading connections of the Waters-Pierce Oil Company and the Standard Oil Company of Indiana in the state. Hadley wanted to know if either concern paid the Terminal Company of St. Louis any sum of money for the privilege of piping its oil across the Mississippi River. In his response to this inquiry, C. P. Eckhardt, manager of the Waters-Pierce Company in St. Louis, admitted that the Standard Oil Company did not come into competition with Waters-Pierce in St. Louis, although it did compete in Sedalia, Clinton, and other towns in Missouri. But he could not explain why St. Louis was the only large city in the country in which Standard Oil did not compete for business. This information merely piqued Hadley's desire to know more, and he continued to search for information. Hadley soon found that Standard Oil did not have an agency in St. Louis, and that Waters-Pierce did not do business in Kansas City. He also discovered that the oil rates from Kansas City to St. Louis was 17 cents, but 22 cents in the opposite direction. The difference, he found, was due to the fact that the Standard had a refinery in Kansas City from which it shipped oil to St. Louis, while in St. Louis the only refinery was an independent with independent clients in Kansas City. Hadley had discovered that the Standard and Waters-Pierce Companies divided the territory in Missouri, and manipulated oil freight charges to damage the independent trade. He also uncovered information to suggest that a third company, Republic Oil, which professed to be an independent, was in reality a Standard Oil subsidiary. Apparently the Republic Oil Company had been created to make a show of competition where none existed, and to sell oil at prices fixed by the Standard Oil Company. On March 29, 1905, Hadley concluded that sufficient evidence existed to file suit charging the three companies with having entered into a combination in violation of the state's antitrust law, and that the companies be ousted from doing business in Missouri.[27]

On June 20, 1905, Attorney General Hadley set out to prove publicly that the State of Missouri was under Standard Oil control. Hearings began in St. Louis on that date before Judge Robert Anthony, appointed by the state supreme court to hear testimony. A. L. Stocke, secretary of the St. Louis Oil Company, an independent concern, testified that the territory in Missouri had been divided by the Standard-Waters-Pierce-Republic group, and that he had actually been asked to enter into an agreement with them. He stated that his company could not do business in some sections of the state because freight rates were too high. In some parts of the state his company came into competition with the Standard, and in some parts with the Waters-Pierce Company. He said that the Standard controlled the northern half of the state and Waters-Pierce the southern half. Where anti-monopoly prejudice against these two concerns was strong, the Republic controlled the territory of the so-called "dissatisfied trade." The witness testified that consumers bought oil from the Republic without suspecting that it was part of a combine. Stocke stated that the Republic Company had been formerly known as the Scofield, Schumer, and Teagle Company, but as soon as the name was changed they attempted to make "terrific drives at our business."[28] H. J. Cohn, salesman for the St. Louis oil firm of George P. Jones and Company, confirmed the remarks made by Stocke, but informed the attorney general that the three companies in mention also employed a common auditor. George N. Hendricks, employed from 1880–1904 by the Waters-Pierce Company, testified that he had referred all reports of Waters-

Pierce business to the vice president of the company at 26 Broadway, New York City, the corporate headquarters of the Standard Oil Company. This information was almost as fascinating as that which placed the main office of the Republic Oil Company at 75 New Street, New York City, which happened to be the rear entrance to the main Standard Oil offices at 26 Broadway. Hendricks also stated that the Waters-Pierce Company received oil in Union (Standard) tank cars in East St. Louis, piped it to St. Louis, and sent it out from there in Waters-Pierce cars.[29]

Other witnesses testified that the Standard had a "partner" in its marketing maneuvers. L. C. Lohman, for thirty years an independent oil dealer in Jefferson City, implied that the Standard operated in collusion with the railroads. He said that he had been forced to abandon his patronage of independent oil companies because the Missouri Pacific, the Missouri, Kansas and Texas, and the Chicago and Alton Railroads had refused to accept shipments to him from independent companies. In his opinion the Waters-Pierce Company had instructed the railroads to take that action. W. N. Davis, formerly an agent for the Consolidated Tank Line Company (Standard), testified that the Consolidated always received information on Standard competitors from the railroads. The company, he said, forwarded this information to agents in the districts of competitors with instructions to get their business by cutting rates. The investigation, which adjourned temporarily in July, had provided damaging evidence. Clearly the Standard Oil Company possessed the economic power to reach into every town or village in a state like Missouri and control the consumption of oil. Neither the consumer nor the independent dealer could exercise his independent right of bargain. The buyer was at the mercy of the seller, and the seller was a monopoly.[30]

The public in the Midwest continued to get a lesson in the marketing methods of a giant corporation when the Missouri hearings resumed in October, 1905. On October 16, Charles B. Collins, former financial secretary to Waters-Pierce president Henry Clay Pierce, testified that two-thirds of the profits of that company flowed into the offices of the Standard Oil Company at 26 Broadway. This revelation implied Standard financially controlled Waters-Pierce. Hadley was of the opinion that the Standard had forced the Waters-Pierce Company to sell to it after that company had incurred debt obligations that it was unable to meet because of stock market manipulations by the Standard Oil people. This allusion to the manipulative power possessed by Standard wealth would find much acceptance during the Panic of 1907. William A. Morgan, former manager of the Standard Oil Company at Sedalia, Missouri, testified that the Standard issued orders to its agents to undersell and destroy competition at all costs. If price cutting proved to be an insufficient tool against competition, the witness stated that the company had furnished him with barrel gauges by which he would be able to show customers that a competitor sold "short" barrels. T. R. Hopkins, a local agent for the Waters-Pierce Company, testified that to meet competition his employer offered rebates to patrons of independent salesmen, while maintaining prices to the general public.[31]

In Missouri much of the general "oil-consuming" public lived in rural areas, and rural Missourians appeared to be intensely interested in the proceedings. Oil was an important product of consumption as it served as the farmer's light and gasoline as his summer fuel in many places. Most rural newspapers closely followed the hearings being conducted in Missouri. Editors kept their readers well informed while availing themselves of an opportunity for critical comment. To the *Joplin News Herald*, the investigation had shown much of the methods of the Standard that were "never suggested by . . . Miss Tarbell; facts that come home more directly to the people of Missouri than any . . . treacheries with Eastern oil operators." And the editors of the *News Herald* were undoubtedly speaking for newspaper and public as they stated that Hadley's probe dealt with "skinning the man who buys his gallon can of coal oil for his lamp or the woman who uses a gasoline stove and pays a needlessly high price for her fuel." The people knew they were paying dear for kerosene because competition had been crushed, and a feeling of resentment had been building over the years. The Standard had gouged them, the Republic had tricked them, but when Henry H. Rogers scorned them they rallied behind their various state representatives and legal prosecutors.[32]

On January 5, 1906, Hadley moved the hearings to New York

City and inadvertently aroused popular opinion on a national scale. Hadley intended to use his broadest investigative prerogative to strengthen the evidence of common ownership, and to establish the intent of that ownership, by the three oil companies named in the Missouri suit. He obtained the appointment of a special commissioner in New York and issued subpoenas for numerous Standard Oil officials. Henry H. Rogers, William G. Rockefeller, and John D. Archbold were among the most notable of those served. But Hadley quickly encountered difficulty. The witnesses were defiant and, on "advice of counsel," they refused to answer questions put to them. In the person of Rogers, defiance changed to arrogance. As a director of the Standard Oil Company, he refused to admit that he knew where Standard Oil's main offices were located, and he insulted the Missouri Supreme Court by stating his indifference to their desire to obtain testimony.[33] On one occasion Rogers flippantly remarked that "his interest in refining oil was comparable to his interest in Carrie Nation."[34]

The results were devastating. The national press seized the opportunity to sensationalize this open contempt for the law, and praised Hadley as the valiant young lawman from the West who had stormed the lion in his den. The *Chicago News* entitled its editorial "Insults From Rogers" and commented: "There is a widespread and growing impression in this country that certain men made arrogant by the possession of great wealth and the power which it brings, are disposed to consider themselves superior to the law."[35] Other newspapers ran similar editorials. The banner of the *Philadelphia Record* reported "Standard Oil Insolence," the editors of the *New York Press* proclaimed "Cheap and Coarse Jests," and the *St. Joseph (Missouri) News Press* attracted the reader's attention with a headline of "Presumptuous Impudence."[36] The publicity given the hearings in New York had been invaluable. Hadley believed the attitude assumed by the corporation would "be of great help to the State of Missouri in its future efforts to check the aggressions of the Standard Oil Company."[37] The Missouri Attorney General received hundreds of letters from current and former employees of the Standard and from others wishing to volunteer testimony and promising leads to further information.[38]

The Missouri hearings, and the accompanying popular reaction, provided a basis and a mood for a series of legal actions in other states during the spring and summer of 1906. Wade H. Ellis, the Attorney General of Ohio, made arrangements to join Missouri in the Standard Oil fight, and explored the possibility of bringing suit under Ohio's antitrust law.[39] In Toledo, Ohio, ouster proceedings were filed in the Circuit Court against the Standard Oil Company and seventeen affiliated companies, including oil and pipe line companies, and the Lake Shore, Hocking Valley, Toledo, and Ohio Central Railroads. Jewell P. Lightfoot, Assistant Attorney General from Texas, initiated suits to oust the Waters-Pierce Company, alleging violations of the Texas antitrust laws of 1899 and 1903. Lightfoot attended many of the Missouri hearings expressly to hear the testimony of Henry Clay Pierce. The Texas suit asked for penalties totaling $5,228,400 for alleged violations of the law over a six-year period.[40] Arkansas Attorney General Robert Lee Rogers also filed suit against the Waters-Pierce Company, alleging a conspiracy to control the output and price of oil. He charged that Waters-Pierce operated in conjunction with the Standard Oil Company and the Republic Oil Company, and had violated the Arkansas antitrust law by being a member of a combine. Damages were asked in the sum of $2,000,000. Kansas also took part in this legal assault upon the Standard at the state level. Attorney General C. C. Coleman filed *quo warranto* proceedings against the Standard Oil Company of Indiana, the Standard Oil Company of Kansas, and the Prairie Oil and Gas Company for antitrust violations.[41]

The federal government had been closely watching the progress of the various state investigations, and slowly obtained results from the work of its own legal apparatus. On May 2, 1906, the commissioner of corporations issued his Report on the Transportation of Petroleum. The Bureau of Corporations, under the direction of James R. Garfield, had been at work for over a year and had found numerous abuses. The Bureau discovered that railroads had granted secret rates to the Standard that enabled it to reach markets at advantages in costs of transportation that often ranged as high as from one to one and a half cents per gallon. This advantageous situation allowed the Standard to control the petroleum market. In addition, the report cited examples of local discrimination in published rates that were intended to favor shipping points where only the Standard had established refineries. Two days later President Roosevelt took advantage of the occasion to publicly denounce the Standard in his message transmitting the Garfield Report to Congress. In his message Roosevelt announced that action would be taken by the Department of Justice to punish carriers for granting and the Standard Oil Company for receiving special rate privileges. Then, on August 27, 1906, the U.S. District Court of Northern Illinois returned 1,903 indictments against the Standard Oil Company of Indiana on criminal charges of accepting unlawful discriminations in transportation. But the federal government also had hopes of prosecuting under the Sherman Act, and, in September, the Justice Department sent Charles Conners to Jefferson City to talk to Attorney General Hadley. Conners remained in the state capital for two weeks, gathering evidence to be used in a federal suit against the Standard Oil Company. Finally, on November 15, 1906, the federal government filed a petition in equity against the Standard Oil Company of New Jersey and its seventy constituent corporations and partnerships in the Eastern District Circuit of Missouri. The petition alleged that a combination and conspiracy in restraint of trade had been created in violation of the Sherman Act, and asked for a dissolution of the combine.[42]

In September, 1906, an incident occurred during the Missouri investigation that underscored the issue of special privilege involved, further agitated the popular mood, and pointed out the need for tougher penalties under the state antitrust laws. The frequency and range of the attacks on the Standard had been increasing, but penalties in almost all state cases involved merely a fine and the threat of being ousted from doing business in that state. A fine of perhaps $5,000 might have seemed like a lot to workers, farmers, consumers, taxpayers, and small businessmen, but stood for little on the scale of corporate profits. Attorney General Hadley was aware of the problem and, as the 1906 political campaign approached, he suggested a solution: "In Missouri we need a law that will send the trust barons to jail when they violate the law. The Missouri legislature has done nothing in the last twenty years towards the enactment of such a statute."[43] A month later, during the testimony of

Henry Clay Pierce, a great many more people began to see the necessity of such an argument. During the course of the hearing Pierce testified that his company sometimes made as much as a 700 percent profit, and that the average was about 400 percent. To consumers this was an outrage. In a letter to the editor of the *Post-Dispatch* one reader commented that this would be one of the factors that would "inevitably make for public ownership." Such information would force people to raise critical questions. "Why should such enormous profits go to a few? Why should they not be distributed among the people who, as consumers, give all value to the products?"[44] That same day the newspaper editorialized on the 700 percent profit and referred to it as "an advertisement of the cost of monopoly to the people."[45] Solutions to the problem—public ownership, federal-state regulation, or trust busting—undoubtedly differed, but people could agree that the problem was privilege. The political and legal system would have to produce tougher antitrust laws, convictions, and heavier fines to curb the menace of monopoly.

As Missouri's investigation of the Standard neared a conclusion, the Missouri legislature responded to public pressure and the urgings of Attorney General Hadley and pressed for tougher antitrust legislation. When the legislature met in January, 1907, a new antitrust law was introduced. In addition, Governor Joseph W. Folk promoted his own anti-discrimination bill. The measure provided that no firm or corporation could sell its products higher in one part of the state than in another, costs of transportation being considered. Aimed directly at the Standard Oil Company, the act prohibited the existing sliding schedule of rates on oil to Missouri consumers under penalty of a $1,000 fine for each violation. The legislature acted quickly and, on March 19, 1907, passed both the anti-discrimination and the amended antitrust statutes. The revised section of the antitrust law stated that violations would be declared a felony. In addition to a fine any person violating the provisions of the act could be convicted and punished by imprisonment for up to five years. These actions occurred concurrently with summations in the Standard Oil hearings. After listening to the closing arguments of Attorney General Hadley and the attorneys for the Standard, Special Commissioner Robert Anthony filed his report with the state supreme court, and pointed out sweeping violations of Missouri's antitrust law. Anthony concluded that the operation of the Standard in Missouri involved "a conspiracy formed to control prices and throttle competition."[46]

For the first time in its existence the Standard experienced a sustained assault upon all facets of its operations, an assault that challenged the assumptions as well as the practices of monopoly. By the spring of 1907, at least eight states threatened the Standard Oil Company with antitrust suits. The federal government took part as well, contesting the Standard over antitrust and railroad rate infractions. But the worst was yet to come. Beginning with the Special Commissioner's Report in the Missouri case in mid-May, and lasting until the Panic struck the nation in mid-October, 1907, the Standard waged a war for survival. In fact, the confrontation actually began a month before the Missouri hearings ended. On April 14, the U.S. District Court of Northern Illinois returned a guilty verdict on 1,462 of the 1,903 counts that had been charged in August of 1906. Judge Kenesaw Mountain Landis took the amount of the fine under deliberation in Chicago.[47] This action preceded the report of Herbert Knox Smith, the new commissioner of corporations, entitled "Position of the Standard Oil Company in the Petroleum Industry." The report, issued on May 20, found that the Standard, though nominally dissolved in 1892 as an unlawful combination in restraint of trade, had evaded that decree and had continued to operate with substantially the same organization as before. The Standard continued to possess monopoly positions as purchaser of crude oil, owner of pipe lines, and refiner of oil.[48] Two weeks later the State of Texas took the leadership of state antitrust activity away from Missouri, ousting the Waters-Pierce Oil Company from that state and fining the company $1,623,900 for violating Texas laws. This was the largest state fine for corporate misconduct ever recorded. The state followed this action by filing a petition for the appointment of a receiver and for the issuance of an injunction to restrain the company from moving any of its property from the state.[49] Texas took a second unprecedented step when the nation's most drastic state antitrust measure became law on July 12. The new law, known as the Terrell Act, provided that any person who represented as agent or sold goods made by a trust or combine would be deemed guilty of a felony and susceptible to imprisonment for from two to ten years.[50]

As the summer months wore on, the attack upon the Standard in particular, and upon all trusts in general, continued. On August 3, Judge Landis imposed the maximum penalty— $20,000 for each offense—upon the Standard Oil Company, a fine that totaled $29,240,000. In issuing his decision Judge Landis remarked: "The men who thus deliberately violate the law wound society more deeply than does he who counterfeits the coin or who steals letters from the mail."[51] The fine was for violation of the Elkins law of 1903, which sought to prohibit railroads from transporting the goods of a shipper at rates lower than those posted by the road and filed with the Interstate Commerce Commission. The law also prohibited shippers, such as Standard Oil, from receiving such rates. Two days later the Bureau of Corporations released the second "Garfield Report," entitled "Prices and Profits in the Petroleum Industry," to the public. The report concluded that for twenty-five years the Standard had dominated the oil business "by methods economically and morally unjustifiable."[52] The report emphasized the relationship between the price of crude oil and the retail prices charged to consumers, and concluded that consumers had been made to suffer. Petroleum prices to the public had been raised, during the eight years from 1898–1905, "not only absolutely but also relatively to the cost of crude oil."[53] Consumers had gained no advantage from the Standard's superior efficiency. Pipe line transportation and large-scale refining had not led to price reductions.[54]

Coincident with the Landis decision and the Bureau of Corporations report was an abrupt drop in prices on Wall Street. The severity of the decline caused many stocks to fall to their lowest figures in six years.[55] While granting some basis of truth to the argument that court, federal, and state actions had upset the market, "experienced bankers" seemed to be more comfortable with an explanation that placed blame on the unstable position of the world money markets. But the *Nation* admitted that not everyone accepted the explanation of the financial experts. "In some quarters, belief is still held in the old-time tradition of a Wall Street 'object lesson,' by which was meant the sale of stocks by important financiers, with a view to causing demoralization among investors, and thus proving to the public at large the financial results of an objectionable public action."[56] This view was more simply stated in the popular song title "Save Up Your Money, John D. Rockefeller Put The Panic On."[57]

The issue of deliberateness involved in the Wall Street slump was still in doubt when John D. Rockefeller made some threatening remarks during a rare interview given shortly after the Landis decision. When asked his opinion of the effect on the country of the present antitrust actions, Rockefeller commented: "The policy of the present administration toward great business combinations of all kinds has only one result. It means disaster to the country, financial depression and financial chaos."[58] A week later President Roosevelt responded directly to this political strike by the sage of big business and hinted at his own opinion of whether the drop in the stock market was privately induced. In a speech made in Provincetown, Massachusetts, on August 20, Roosevelt stated:

On the New York Stock Exchange the disturbance has been particularly severe . . . it may well be that the determination of the Government, in which it will not waiver, to punish certain malefactors of great wealth, has been responsible for something of the troubles at least to the extent of having caused these men to combine to bring about as much financial stress as they possibly can in order to discredit the policy of the Government and thereby to secure a reversal of that policy so that they may enjoy the fruits of their own evil doings.[59]

Both the Rockefeller interview and the Roosevelt speech were symbolic expressions to the people who had been providing the sustained popular support for the antitrust movement. Rockefeller appealed to the "amoral" priority of economic gain, with economic growth as society's highest goal. As the spokesman for big business, he reminded people that their support for the current political and legal activity caused economic dislocation for business and threatened depression for the rest of society. Roosevelt, on the other hand, sought to arouse the "moral" priority of economic conscience and intensify the antitrust movement. By attempting to expose the self-interest designs of big business, he hoped to lead the crusade in the public interest and direct it against "bad" trusts and monopolies.

Roosevelt had given an indication of his intentions by bold statement, but the various state attorneys general decided upon a more forceful policy of concerted action. On August 12, a preliminary meeting of the leading legal officials of the states actively engaged in antitrust proceedings convened in St. Louis.[60] The plan, outlined in the request for the conference by Attorney General Hadley, called for a national meeting of state attorneys general to provide the opportunity for the exchange of ideas on how states might best assist each other in the battle against trusts. Agenda items included the concern for more uniform state laws, the simultaneous filing of suits against the same offenders, and concerted action against the many subsidiary companies established in the various states. The result of this meeting was the first National Attorneys General Conference, which took place in St. Louis on September 30 and October 1, 1907.[61]

One of the main points under discussion at the conference concerned the desire to shift the emphasis of state prosecutions away from fines, as ultimately the consumer must pay, to that of placing trust magnates in jail. In the opening address to the conference, Assistant Attorney General Lightfoot of Texas agreed with progressive sociologist E. A. Ross that in order to discipline a large industrial combination, the people's legal representatives had to place responsibility upon morally insensitive individuals. Ross was especially concerned with what he perceived as the evolution of a new social type, the "criminaloid." As a consequence of a rapidly changing and increasingly complex economic system, people had become interdependent. In the process, one's vitial interests had been entrusted to others. To Ross, this change threatened the very moral fibre of the nation as it allowed for new forms of wrongdoing, misconduct, and "latter-day sin," which were all connected with money-making. By utilizing the anti-social ethics that characterized the emerging system of industrial capitalism, the new businessman—the criminaloid or modern-day malefactor—trampled the ideals of the nation and did harm to society. The public welfare and the general sense of rights held by the community were disregarded and the public trust betrayed. To meet this new threat, society needed to redefine proper social conduct, expand its definition of crime, and use the law to reinstill social justice by adjusting the magnitude of the punishment to match the lucrative nature of the crime. According to Ross, who may have been influenced by the Standard Oil case in writing *Sin and Society*, the "brake of the law" would never "grip these slippery wheels until prison doors yawn for the convicted officers of lawless corporations."[62] The directors of a corporation had to be held individually accountable for instances of misconduct beneficial to the corporation. Only the threat of such severe legal pressure could insure corporate responsibility. Lightfoot recommended that every state adopt a statute providing for the imprisonment of from two to ten years for every officer, or agent of a corporation convicted of having knowledge of any illegal transaction by the parent company. As justification for the need for such criminal action, Lightfoot offered his opinion that the trusts oppressed the poorer classes, and that unless they were curbed by law, revolution would occur.[63]

The fact that the conference took place at all offered convincing evidence of the degree, especially since the Kansas uprising of 1905, to which the states had moved toward the identification of a common problem and the acceptance of extreme solutions as a community of states.[64] The struggle at the state level against the Standard Oil empire was a significant episode in both the antitrust movement and in progressivisim. Locally, the people of Kansas responded to the operation of a giant industrial combination that exercised its power to control output and prices, production and consumption. They discovered that the Standard had, in effect, the power to control their lives. The struggle spread to Missouri, a state that produced almost no oil at all. There the issue broadened in scope. The people of Missouri reacted to the results and means of monopoly as injured consumers and as incensed citizens. The Standard was a name that represented more than an oil company. It symbolized all the trusts and monopolies against which they had fought. To the people of Missouri, the Standard was the twine trust, the sugar trust, the gas trust, the beef trust, and the streetcar monopoly. The Standard was the unholiest of all soulless corporations.

When the Missouri hearings ventured to New York and confronted corporate arrogance in the person of Henry H. Rogers, the battle became national in scope. To people everywhere, the Standard had placed itself above the law. Newspaper editors and political cartoonists carried national events directly to readers. The elected legal and political officials in the state and federal government responded to the popular mood. They initiated hearings, conducted investigations, and brought legal suits. They levied fines, ousted corporations, and threatened to jail corporate directors. What had begun as an attempt to restore the ideals of community and economic independence within one state, developed into a movement to establish those same ideals among states.

At the end of October, 1907, Attorney General Hadley formally submitted the Standard Oil case to the Missouri Supreme Court. The decision, which ultimately went in favor of the state, was probably the greatest victory for the popular movement against trusts at the state level. Hadley regarded the trial as "the most important that has come before a court in this country since the Dred Scott case."[65] The comparison was significant. True, fundamental constitutional questions were involved, but so too was the issue of basic human freedom.

REGULATION: A MOVEMENT IS CO-OPTED

The Panic of 1907 killed the popular movement against trusts and monopolies. The movement did not die suddenly, nor were its ranks ever totally decimated, but after 1907 trust policy increasingly shifted toward regulation as an alternative and away from earlier popular efforts aimed at dissolution. The panic alarmed businessmen generally, and caused them to search bitterly for an explanation. The suggestions that an inelastic currency, an overextension of credit, the loss of public faith in bankers, loose banking practices, especially among large New York trust companies, and speculation by financiers were the cause of the Panic were certainly unacceptable to members of the larger Eastern business community. Such suggestions implied that the blame for economic collapse lay with business and banker mismanagement. A much better explanation was that antagonistic war against concentrated wealth, carried on by the states and the national government and personified by President Theodore Roosevelt, was the cause of a "crisis in business confidence." The radical enforcement of antitrust suits in such cases as Standard Oil was said to have "destroyed" business confidence, and financiers and large corporations had been "discouraged from participating in new enterprises" because of such a "hostile" economic environment. These developments, went the standard analysis, had caused credit to be tightened and placed new pressures on smaller businessmen. The panic generated a fear among business interests and made them more receptive to a change toward a less severe antitrust policy.[1]

This change in attitude corresponded directly with the severity and length of the panic itself. In the early fall of 1907 businessmen were optimistic. The minor panics in 1901 and 1903 had helped to boost the confidence of many Midwestern businessmen, as those that suffered seemed to have been Eastern speculators. When the Panic of 1907 intensified, most non-Eastern businessmen initially blamed Wall Street. But as the panic lengthened, it became "Roosevelt's Panic." In August of 1907, when Judge Kenesaw Mountain Landis cracked down on the Standard Oil Company and levied his huge fine, business journals generally approved. But by July of 1908, when the Supreme Court overturned the Landis decision and canceled the fine, those same journals enthusiastically supported the higher court's reversal. Aggressive antitrust actions had become unpopular with business interests.[2]

The solution to the trust problem that gained momentum after the Panic of 1907 proved to be that of governmental regulation of corporations. The idea had actually been advanced a few years before, and the person who did most to popularize it was Theodore Roosevelt. Roosevelt had gained a reputation for condemning malefactors of great wealth, but ideologocally he was far more an advocate of regulation than dissolution in his trust policy.

Roosevelt, as President, began to formulate his theory of government regulation as early as his annual message to Congress on December 3, 1901, when he proposed compulsory publicity of corporate earnings. But a cautious pro-business Congress met his proposals with indifference. Over the next few years President Roosevelt stepped up his call for federal regulation of interstate commerce and placed special emphasis on the railroads. In December of 1906, amidst rumors of an impending break in the stock market, Roosevelt submitted a stern message to Congress and declared that all big business was really engaged in interstate commerce and should be brought under control and supervision. In March of 1907, Roosevelt wrote to the Interstate Commerce Commission that he did "not believe in the sweeping and indiscriminate prohibition of all combination which has been so marked and as I think so mischievous a feature of our anti-trust legislation."[3] In point of fact, Roosevelt had actually entered into private agreements with Morgan interests (U.S. Steel in November, 1905 and International Harvester in January, 1907). Such gentlemanly agreements, seeking business-government cooperation instead of an aggressive antitrust policy, were preferred by both parties. Businesses looked for stability and immunity from prosecution as long as they were innocent of flagrant antitrust violations. To this end, they accepted the supervisory role of a strong executive such as Roosevelt, and believed that his word was his bond on policy. Roosevelt, looking for an improved basis for antitrust policy, sought to obtain discretionary power to distinguish between good and bad trusts.[4]

Roosevelt had refused to modify his antagonistic antitrust rhetoric in the face of Rockefeller's accusations during the summer of 1907, but the economic dislocations caused by the panic forced him to alter his stance in order to restore business confidence. During the panic the President, in December of 1907, increased his emphasis on regulation in urging Congress to set up a means of federal supervision of all interstate business. Finally, during the campaign of 1908, the implications of business confidence compelled him to the point where he could argue that the only effective action against large industrial consolidation was to increase "federal control over all combinations . . . instead of relying upon the foolish anti-trust law."[5]

Roosevelt's successor, William H. Taft, never really grasped Roosevelt's more subtle views on the trust question, and modified his program of government regulation of trusts. Somewhat adrift, Taft obtusely wrote to the ex-President: "What we believe in, if I understand it, is the regulation of the business of the trusts as distinguished from its destruction."[6] President Taft never really followed any consistent policy in antitrust affairs, but he did temporarily destroy the system of accommodation by informal understanding that Roosevelt had developed with business (at least with the Morgan interests). Taft opted, instead, to interpret the antitrust law in a strict legal sense. Administration, not innovation, was the key. Once Taft assumed office, his overpowering legal bias compelled him to go beyond his predecessor and initiate many more antitrust suits. However, Taft's public views on the regulation of big business were not substantially different from Roosevelt's. He never really dropped the rhetoric of discretionary regulation, and assisted in publicizing the idea between 1909 and 1912.[7]

The Panic of 1907 also influenced Taft and made him aware of the need to preserve business confidence. In his special message to Congress on January 7, 1910, President Taft struck just such a note for regulation and confidence:

[The] prosecution of corporations whose prosperity or destruction affects the comfort not only of stockholders, but millions of wage-earners, employees, and associated tradesmen must necessarily tend to disturb the confidence of the business community, to dry up the now flowing sources of capital from its places of hoarding, and produce a halt in our present prosperity that will cause suffering and strained circumstances among the innocent many for the faults of the guilty few. The question which I wish in this message to bring clearly to the consideration and discussion of Congress is whether in order to avoid such possible business danger something cannot be done by which these business combinations may be offered a means, without great financial disturbance, of changing the character, organization, and extent of their business into one within the lines of the law under Federal control and supervision, securing compliance with the antitrust statute.[8]

The President pointed out other "failures" of antitrust activity as he argued that federal regulation could protect corporations from "undue interference by the States," and prevent a recurrence of "those abuses [exorbitant fines and revocation of corporate charters] which have arisen under state control."[9] Federal regulation would also eliminate the "conflicting" [non-uniform] antitrust laws of the different states that made it "difficult, if not impossible," for corporations to comply with all of their requirements. Taft also responded to the assertion of dissolution advocates that a proposal of federal incorporation for industrial combinations would furnish them a refuge from which to continue industrial abuses under federal protection. It was here that Taft gave federal regulation its moral equivalent and the force of law. "Reasonable" combinations would not be interfered with, as these concentrations of capital were necessary for the economic development of manufacture, trade, and commerce. However, combinations that monopolized commerce would be prosecuted. The Sherman Act would not be repealed, but, instead, vigorously enforced in a judicious manner. Federal regulation would also be an efficient improvement over state litigation, and the force of judicial decisions would be enhanced by this efficiency.[10]

State-level policymakers listened to the debate and formulated their own interpretations of what "regulation" might entail. To some, regulation promised to be the great antitrust panacea. Business confidence could be restored and economic stability maintained, combinations that monopolized commerce could be prosecuted while those that enhanced trade could be encouraged, and the entire legal process could be made more efficient. To a good party man, admirer of Theodore Roosevelt, and legalist like Republican Attorney General Herbert S. Hadley of Missouri, the idea of regulation seemed worthy of consideration.

Hadley's reputation in the state-level drive to curb trusts and monopolies was crucial, and any change in his position was bound to influence others. It had been Attorney General Hadley's idea to call the first national meeting of attorneys general in St. Louis in late September and early October of 1907. The meeting, which took place just prior to the panic, resulted in several forceful measures calling for the dissolution of trusts and the imprisonment of guilty corporate directors. Hadley, for one, had backed up the resolutions of the conference and the tough public, "trust-busting" utterances of President Roosevelt by successfully closing his arguments in the popular Standard Oil case just a month later. However, over the next year of financial panic Hadley's thinking began to change. At the Second Annual Conference of Attorneys General, which met in Denver, Colorado, on August 20–21, 1908, the first signs of change began to appear. Elected President of the meeting in 1907, Hadley was called upon to deliver the opening address to the second conference. Hadley began on a pessimistic note and lamented that the lack of results secured by state prosecutors over the past year had furnished "an added demonstration of the ineffectiveness of the present methods of litigation for the suppression or punishment of trusts and monopolies." As a legalist, Hadley pointed out some of the defects in current procedures. The law's delay, the "glorification of technicalities," and the inflexible rules of the courts as to procedure and evidence (devised centuries earlier under radically different conditions) all worked to the benefit of the accused corporation, and to the detriment of the various states. In light of these hurdles Hadley suggested a new departure to the conference. The plan described by the attorney general accepted the formation of combinations as inevitable, and even of consolidations in restraint of trade, and substituted regulation in place of prior efforts to punish or suppress. The completion of the plan provided that once a court decided that a trust or combination did exist, the various states had the right to regulate the charges and the conduct of those combinations. This could be accomplished either through legislative action or through the directives of an administrative board. The plan was only a suggestion, but coming when it did, and from a figure such as Hadley, it might well have been given sober consideration by the attending trust fighters who, like Hadley, had originally gathered just one year before to aggressively attack the trusts.[11]

During the fall of 1908, Hadley's career underwent its own political transformation as his term as attorney general ended and his successful quest for the governorship began. In the process, his advocacy of the regulation of trusts intensified. During the campaign Hadley described to Missourians the merits of regulation over the inefficiency of the old methods of antitrust enforcement. The example that Hadley used was the insurance business. The Insurance Trust had been "defeated" by former Attorney General Edward C. Crow in 1899 when seventy-three participants in the St. Joseph Social Club had been fined $1,000 each and the St. Louis and Kansas City rating boards disbanded. But sometime after 1906 renewed complaints over insurance rates began to be heard. This led Hadley to begin his own investigation which resulted in proceedings against sixty-nine fire insurance companies doing business in Missouri. He heard testimony and investigated, and became satisfied that the earlier insurance suit had not corrected abuses in the fire insurance business. The attorney general found that rates were fixed arbitrarily and determined with little regard to the hazard of risk involved. At the conclusion of testimony the various insurance companies sought to negotiate a settlement of the litigation. Hadley informed them that if they re-rated all property in the state (presumably in conjunction with and under the direction of the State Superintendent of Insurance) on a scientific, standardized basis according to the hazard of risk involved, he would hold the suit in abeyance. The readjustment of rates in the city and county of St. Louis resulted in reductions in rates on business property of from 20 to 40 percent, and projections for the rest of the state showed an average fire insurance rate reduction of 10 percent. To Hadley, state regulation was a viable antitrust alternative: "Where is the man not blinded by partisan prejudice who would hesitate to admit that this is a better plan of procedure than to secure the imposition of a fine which the defendants could in a few months recoup by an advance in charges."[12]

Governor Hadley continued to refine and publicize his commitment to state regulation of trusts. During his inaugural address the new governor sought to calm any fears that corporations might have in regard to the new move towards state regulation. Corporations had rights too, and should in no way be deprived, by either the courts or public officials, of a reasonable return on the value of their investments. Regulation and control should only be used when conditions clearly justified it. This would be done when restraints in trade clearly hurt smaller manufacturers or producers, or when fixed or artificially raised prices operated to the detriment of consumers. The mere potential to restrain trade, fix prices, or control the market would not be interfered with as it had in earlier antitrust cases. In other words, good trusts—those that provided efficient and inventive production and justifiable prices in exchange for market control—would be left alone. However, this method still left unanswered precisely how terms such as "efficient," "inventive," and "justifiable" would be determined within the regulatory context. The rather autocratic thrust of this solution was a far cry from the more democratic nature of the earlier, popular antitrust movements which premised actions on considerations of rights and privileges.[13]

Hadley was certainly aware of the effects of the Panic of 1907 on business conditions generally, and of the popular argument among businessmen that antagonistic antitrust proceedings had contributed to that instability. By February of 1909, he began to see the possible validity of such an argument within his own state-bounded economic domain. When the Standard Oil Company, which had been formally ousted from Missouri in December of 1908, proposed to the state supreme court that it be allowed to continue to do business in Missouri under state supervision, Hadley was sympathetic. Perhaps the judgments in the antitrust cases were too harsh. Perhaps Hadley's ouster of Standard Oil from Missouri could be just as detrimental for his state's economy as the Landis decision appeared to many national businessmen to be on the nation's economy. In a way, Hadley was a victim of his new political role. As governor it was his job to "boost" his state, to attract business, to encourage economic growth and development. As the state's chief administrator he was certainly aware of the "spinoffs" or the larger implications of the pro-business argument. Business meant sales, jobs, and increased revenue for the state through taxes and licenses. If the outlines of this new position were just being formed in Hadley's mind in January and February of 1909, he had at least set his political wheels on a more conservative track. The beginning of Hadley's professional and intellectual conversion loosened from the popular antitrust movement in Missouri one of its leaders, and promised to give to it its own state-level agent of co-optation.[14]

In early 1909, Governor Hadley had only just started on the path of state regulation. He still needed time to refine his ideas, time to check the political climate and test the sentiments of his constituency, and time to observe the reactions of business to continued antitrust prosecutions. On February 26, 1909, Hadley described the direction of his thinking in a letter to President Taft in which he stated that he was attempting to put into statutory law some of the opinions he had acquired through his experience in antitrust legislation. Conceding that existing laws were deficient in addressing certain restraints in competition, Hadley advanced his own remedy: "A business which, by reason of size or plan of organization, controls the price of any commodity is, in law, impressed with a public use and is, therefore, subject to regulation by the state or national government, and is a public service corporation."[15] Enthusiastic in his ideas, Hadley urged the legislature to pass laws that would give state officials discretionary power to regulate the charges and conduct of businesses which were, in effect, monopolies. Confident of his direction he carried his appeal to the people during his speaking tour of Chatauquas in the summer of 1909. To understand the attitudes of business, he listened to the reactions of business and the courts to continued antitrust activity that came to him during the prosecution of Missouri's suit against the International Harvester Corporation.[16]

The International Harvester case provides an excellent example of an antitrust action that originated in an angry mood of dissolution and ended in a more conciliatory temper of regulation. In March of 1907, the Missouri House of Representatives instructed Attorney General Hadley to investigate the Harvester Trust.[17] The lower house of the General Assembly took the action after receiving complaints from farmers from around the state. The increased costs of farm implements and the lack of competition in the business, which compelled farmers to pay trust prices, formed the basis of the grievances. Upon investigation, Hadley found that the International Harvester Company had organized in 1902 as a consolidation of the five principal manufacturers of harvesting machines in the United States.[18] On June 2, 1902, Cyrus H. McCormick went to financial promoter George W. Perkins of the firm of J. P. Morgan and Company to see if he could suggest a way of relieving competitive conditions, which, to McCormick, were "fierce," "unbusinesslike," and "fraught with evil from the viewpoint of the manufacturers." Perkins then conceived of the idea of forming a holding company, with each of the five major companies in the industry becoming a part. The holding company, a corporation chartered in New Jersey and known as the International Harvester Company, was formalized on August 12, 1902, and capitalized at $120,000,000. Such a large corporation could not obtain a license under Missouri law, so the International Harvester Company of America was formed as a selling agent to evade the laws of the state. Monopoly control over the sale of binders in Missouri resulted from the consolidation, and on these grounds Attorney General Hadley brought ouster proceedings against the alleged trust on November 12, 1907.[19]

Hadley's Democratic successor as attorney general, Elliott W. Major, assumed the task of completing the Harvester suit. Major strengthened the case by obtaining damaging testimony from a number of implement dealers and further details of the alleged combine from George W. Perkins himself. The implement dealers testified that the Harvester Trust had coerced them to quit handling the machines of independent companies and that prices had been advanced by the trust. Perkins admitted that the new corporation (International Harvester Company of New Jersey) continued to manufacture the machines of all the firms in the holding company (preserving their separate makes and identities), sold them at a uniform price, and that competition amongst the member companies and the independent companies purchased since 1902 had been eliminated. The International Harvester Company did 85 percent of the harvesting machine business not only in Missouri, but in the entire United States. In its own defense the International contended that it handled twenty-one lines of business, did the greater part of the business in only two lines (mowers and binders), sold farm implements at reasonable prices, and had not violated the Missouri antitrust law.[20]

Special Commissioner Theodore Brace heard the evidence and, on September 7, 1910, issued his report to the state supreme court in which he sided with the state. Judge Brace found that the International Harvester Company of New Jersey had been organized for the purpose of destroying competition, had achieved a monopoly in the manufacture and sale of harvesting machinery, and that its distributing agent was subject to ouster under the Missouri antitrust law. On November 14, 1911, the Missouri Supreme Court finally upheld the report of the special commissioner and imposed a fine of $50,000 (later reduced to $25,000) on the International Harvester Company of America. The court also stipulated that if the Missouri corporation paid the fine, separated itself from the parent company, filed a statement of its business operations, and proved to the court that it would obey Missouri laws in the future, it would be permitted to continue to do business in the state. The inclusion of this latter provision had been standard practice in most Missouri antitrust decisions, but the court appeared to be closely following political pronouncements at the national and state levels as it moved beyond procedural considerations to assistance in the implementation of new antitrust policy structured around the principle of regulation.[21]

If Attorney General Major's prosecution of the Missouri suit can be seen as a continued appeal for aggressive antitrust prosecution, the defense and the decision of the court were implicit requests for the need of some sort of state or federal regulation or perhaps even a federal incorporation law. When the International Harvester Company filed its brief with the Missouri Supreme Court in March, 1911, it challenged the report of the special commissioner. The company presented evidence from seventy-three Missouri retailers to prove that competition existed in its line of business. The International also denied that there was any basis for the argument that it was the "irresistible tendency" of trusts to raise selling prices, to lower the prices on raw materials, to reduce the quality of manufactured products, and to depress wages. In the minds of company directors, none of those results followed upon its organization.[22]

The argument of the company was bold, but the court found it to be not altogether untrue. The court agreed with the state that the International had organized to restrict competition in the sale of binders, mowers, and reapers, and had managed to control 80 to 90 percent of the farm implement business. The company compelled its agents to take their machines at set figures and to sell them at fixed prices. But the court also found that the Harvester Trust had not adversely affected prices. In fact, in the first year after the finalization of the consolidation agreement, prices to consumers actually decreased. Thereafter, there was a small increase in price levels, but not nearly equal to the increases in the costs of materials and labor. The court found the combine to be, in its words, "beneficial to the community." Prices were not only held down in proportion to increases in the cost of production, but independent manufacturers had not been injured and the power of the company had not been used to oppress or injure farmers who were its customers. It was on this last point, however, that the court hinged its decision. The consolidation arrangement had been designed to thwart competition, and, as such, provided the combine with an unlimited potential to drive other competitors from the field and oppress farmers. The trust had violated the letter of the law and was convicted. But to businessmen, and to conservative judicial officials who had moved toward a business and economic stability focus in rendering their decisions, the Harvester case served as another prime example of a "beneficial" trust that had been harshly punished by an inflexible antitrust statute.[23]

In many ways the Missouri suit was a continuation of Kansas' battle with the same corporation which ended in February of 1910. The Kansas Supreme Court also returned a limited ouster decision against the International. In its decision the court stated that it had found evidence to justify the forfeiture of the defendant's charter and right to conduct business in Kansas. But the court did not deem such punitive action to be either "necessary or expedient" at the present time. As the volume of business in harvester machinery transacted in Kansas was sufficient enough to make it a matter of public concern "and a proper subject for regulation," the court formally reserved the right to regulate the trust in the future, to take up complaints, and to settle them as it determined.[24] The International Harvester case was an important episode in the antitrust movement at the state level, and a contributing element in the shift in the attitudes of policymakers toward the idea of regulation.

Governor Hadley, who had initiated action against the same combine in Missouri, agreed with the Missouri court when it reached a decision similar to that arrived at in Kansas. Hadley accepted the claims of the Harvester Company, and the opinion of the court, that increased prices of materials and labor justified any increases in the prices of harvesting machinery. He also agreed with the court that the final question at issue was solely one of law. But an acceptance of the first condition and an agreement with the second basic point of law undoubtedly left Hadley with the same tormented feeling that he had exuded in his first inaugural address. Business regarded free and unrestricted competition as a misfortune and an evil, but the law could only denounce any agreement that tended to prevent it as a crime. There remained in his mind that basic conflict between the "rules of business and the laws of men."[25]

The decision in the Missouri Harvester case also renewed pressures for a shift toward the idea of regulation of some sort at the national level as well. Two weeks after the Missouri decision, George W. Perkins met privately with President Taft to discuss commercial and industrial conditions and possibly to plead for a return to the concept of "private arrangements" utilized earlier by Roosevelt in connection with Morgan interests.[26] Though the exact details of the talk were not disclosed, Perkins did grant an interview to the *St. Louis Post-Dispatch* in which he discussed his commercial opinions. It would not be too presumptuous to suppose that similar points had been impressed upon President Taft, and that Perkins, in presenting his case, hoped to evade possible federal prosecution. Perkins stressed that it should be the policy of government to curb large-scale industrial consolidations, not to destroy them. Aggressive antitrust prosecutions, in his opinion, weakened business confidence. What was needed, he suggested, was a federal license for corporations doing interstate business. An interstate business could apply for a federal license and get it by showing how its business was capitalized, what its profits were, what compensation it paid to labor, and at what prices it sold its goods to the public. With such a device business could be built up, not torn down.[27]

Three days after the Perkins interview the *Independent* published an editorial that supported the idea of federal regulation and used the Missouri case as supporting evidence. The editors, like the court and Governor Hadley, examined the evidence and found economic benefits. The International had kept prices down relative to production costs, had extended its business into other lines of farm implements and, in doing so, had contributed to a competitive situation that benefited farmers. It had also improved the quality of its manufactures and reduced the items of repair material which placed them in closer reach of the farmer. Had the public interest been served in the enforcement of the Missouri antitrust statute? The *Independent* did not seem to think so and rhetorically asked if it would not be better for the public interest to retain the benefits of big business and still, "by some official influence," prevent a misuse of economic power? Then, more specifically, the editors suggested: "Ought there not be a Federal Interstate Trade Commission, by which the power may be controlled and regulated?"[28] The answer to that question to those at the top levels of the economic system might well have been yes. Cutthroat competition could be eliminated, stability brought to the marketplace, and growth and profits guaranteed. A poll conducted by the National Civic Federation in November, 1911, among businessmen, professional men, and labor leaders, found that those groups favored a national incorporation law by a ratio of 4 to 1. They rejected the idea of returning to the "old competitive methods of business" by an even greater margin.[29]

The larger businesses and the policymakers that favored regulation, and the economic stability that it promised to bring, sought to persuade others by appealing to the basic economic self-interests of individuals. They hinted to consumers and taxpayers that prices and taxes might increase. They lectured small retailers on the need to think like "businessmen" and to value the goal of economic stability. And they frightened workers with the threat of layoffs and lost jobs. This organized effort of persuasion on the part of businessmen, and by policymakers sympathetic to business interests, was fairly successful. The public was pulled along behind a vague regulatory panacea by a form of economic intimidation that was not always subtle. At each step along the way they forfeited a degree of personal control over the very industrial consolidations against which, for twenty-five years, they had struggled so valiantly. In place of this personal control, the corporation imposed its own form of regulatory control by promising people security. Prices and taxes could be kept at moderate levels, small retailers would be allowed to compete, and labor would be allowed to work only if people followed corporate guidelines that facilitated economic growth and stability.

Missouri's continued dealings with the Standard Oil Company offers an excellent example of the methods used by one large corporation, and its commercial allies, to convince the people of an active antitrust state that regulation was in their best interests. The Standard Oil Company had been formally ousted from Missouri in December of 1908, but continued court appeals had delayed the final ouster decree. Early in 1913 the Standard began to impress upon Kansas Citians the adverse economic results that such a decision would mean to them as consumers, taxpayers, small retailers, and workers. The Standard undoubtedly hoped that such economic coercion would provoke public and commercial pressure upon the state legislature to annul the ouster decision. The Standard's most significant economic asset to Missourians was its large oil refinery at Sugar Creek, located very near Kansas City. During the legislative session of 1913, rumors began to circulate that the Standard intended to dismantle its Sugar Creek refinery. Such a rumor especially alarmed the Commercial Club of Kansas City, and it used the newspapers in Kansas City to present its argument.[30] Businessmen regarded fuel oil as a necessity to at least 400 leading Kansas City concerns which employed over 50,000 persons, and over 5,000 homes in Kansas City depended on oil fuel for heat and light. They argued that independent oil dealers would not be able to provide a regular supply of oil in sufficient quantities to meet the needs of local consumers. A switch to the use of coal would be necessitated. The estimated costs of changing heating plants and machinery reached $150,000. Schools and office buildings would have to be converted to coal and conversion would cause plants to close for months and workers to be laid off. A smoke nuisance and a dirtier city would result. The Standard Oil Company contributed to the argument by announcing its intention (if allowed to remain in the state) to double the existing refinery capacity at Sugar Creek. A supportive press in Kansas City quickly pointed out that if the state failed to allow it to do so, it would cause the loss of $2,000,000 worth of construction work for Kansas City.[31]

A view of the larger Kansas City and Sugar Creek communities shows that a mutuality of economic interest existed. The economic forecast from Sugar Creek was bleak. Sugar Creek was a thriving little town of 1,200 inhabitants who had, in the nine years that the Standard had been there, built homes, schools, churches, and businesses. Workers and merchants totally depended upon the Sugar Creek refinery for their livelihood. After the announcement by the Standard that plant capacity would be doubled, boosters in Sugar Creek could surely have been optimistic about the future growth of their community. But if the state ousted the Standard and the Standard dismantled its refinery, Sugar Creek would be ruined. Over $500,000 in homes and stores would be lost, and the citizens impoverished. Consumers who felt that they might be asked to accept higher fuel costs, taxpayers who might be forced to pay the costs of converting municipal facilities, and workers who might be facing unemployment acquiesced to the enthusiastic appeals of the Commercial Club and Sugar Creek. Supported by the unanimous resolutions of the Commercial Club of Independence, the upper house of the Common Council of Kansas City, and the county court, they applied pressure to the state legislature to prevent the ouster of Standard Oil. An outspoken, and in some cases influential, portion of the public appeared ready for some change in existing antitrust policy. As one businessman stated, "whatever the proper remedy for unlawful trusts may be, the infliction of additional injury on the public is not the proper remedy."[32]

State Senator Michael E. Casey of Kansas City introduced a bill in the Missouri legislature to annul the ouster of the Standard Oil Company, and the debate that followed centered around the merits of "busting" as opposed to "regulation" of trusts.[33] The proponents of leniency for the Standard presented the strongest case and, in their defense, they utilized all the regulatory arguments. The prosecution and dissolution of trusts, said the advocates of regulation, had not accomplished any results other than to curb to a limited extent the tendency to consolidate. Ineffective antitrust laws tended to create unsettled conditions within the business community which restricted economic growth. As with the pleas for the homes of the working people at Sugar Creek, aggressive antitrust statutes could also cause severe economic hardship. As stated by the *Kansas City Star*: "The question is becoming more and more important daily whether regulation and supervision of big corporations by the government will produce better results for the entire country than fruitless efforts at dissolution."[34] Ex-Governor Hadley agreed and stated that "no satisfactory results have been obtained in a concrete way. We have been using blank cartridges in a sham battle."[35]

Regulation, on the other hand, could accomplish everything that dissolution had promised, and more efficiently. The criminal provisions and monetary penalties in the law could be maintained, but they would be reserved for "bad" trusts and flagrant violations. Lengthy court suits would be eliminated by the constant vigilance of a regulatory agency or commission, and the open disclosure of corporate dealings would ease the burden of regulation. Most important for business, economic waste would be prevented and economic growth stimulated. Ex-Governor Hadley concurred on this last point and lent his support to the proponents of regulation: "Wherever the choice must be between punishment for past offenses and the correction of conditions by re-establishing competition, the latter is the object and result which should be of first concern."[36] The outlines of the regulatory position that were just being formed in his mind in 1908–1909 had sharpened by 1913. He was now totally in step with the march toward regulation and reminded Missourians that they still lived in one of the most undeveloped states in the Mississippi Valley. With that fact in mind, Hadley supported a policy that would "encourage business interests to come here and aid in the work of developing the undeveloped resources of the State, instead of pursuing a policy of antagonism which will tend to prevent them from doing so."[37] The rules of business were coming to triumph over the laws of men.[38]

The forces for regulation managed to get the Standard Oil measure passed, but not without some resistance.[39] Representative Charles M. Hay, a Democrat from rural Calloway County, appealed to a culture that still understood the importance of traditional, democratic values. Speaking for the dissenters who failed to see the benefits in this legislative recall of a judicial decision, Hay referred to the bill as an admission of democracy's defeat. Those who supported the bill were in fact saying to the trust: "Go ahead; violate the law, and we won't punish you or drive you out because we can't get along without you."[40] Governor Elliott W. Major gave the opposition temporary succor by vetoing the bill, leaving the Missouri Supreme Court to decide whether or not to modify its pending ouster decree. The governor stood firm on the principle that the bill would destroy Missouri's proven antitrust statute, "blunt the point of the weapon and take from it its keen edge."[41] However, the business interests of the state successfully petitioned the state supreme court to allow the Standard Oil Company of Indiana to resume business in Missouri. The order rested upon the condition that the company would continue to operate as an independent, and that it would submit to constant supervision and regulation by the court. The Supreme Court in Missouri had assumed the role of an administrative agency, a role for which it was not really suited. But the precedent of regulation had been established. Only minor legislative adjustments remained before the regulation of corporations could be independently supervised by a federal or state agency, board, or commission.[42]

It should not be assumed that between 1907 and 1913 everyone made the transition from aggressive advocate of the enforcement of antitrust statutes to proponent of state and federal regulation. Some politicians, especially those in the Southwest where antitrust activity had been particularly strong, remained adamant in their positions. Attorney General William F. Kirby of Arkansas could state that he still believed in the "absolute annihilation of trusts." Attorney General Robert V. Davidson of Texas still could not find any difference between "good" trusts and "bad" trusts, "[a] white horse is the same as a black horse; they both kick." Assistant Attorney General Jewel P. Lightfoot of Texas, the state's official trust destroyer, surveyed the commercial situation and showed his strong anti-corporate agrarian roots: "Our entire business world is on an illegal basis. Americans are becoming cogs in a great national organization of commerce. In Texas we prefer to be free—to be independent, even if we have to get back to the sickle and the hoe." Former Texas Attorney General Martin M. Crane supported him on that point and stated: "We want to return to the business conditions of 1880. Our political purpose is to give every small man a chance." Fred C. Jackson, the Attorney General of Kansas, strongly opposed Roosevelt's trust policy, stating that he could "recognize no such thing as a good combination" and that it was a "serious mistake" to declare that any combine could be a national benefit. The Kansas trust-fighters and their neighbors were "out against commercialism." To speak of a good combination was "absurd." "As well might you refer to a 'good' burglar! Every combination was 'conceived in sin and born in iniquity.' "[43]

Trust fighters, like Standard Oil's nemesis Ida M. Tarbell, also refused to alter their aggressive approach to the trust question, and warned fellow muckrakers what was in store for them if they did. In an enlightening letter written to colleague Ray Stannard Baker, one sympathetic to the idea of establishing an independent regulatory commission with broad power to control industrial trade, Tarbell chose to take issue on the topic of trusts. She argued that "monopolistic features" could be abolished, and wrote Baker: "You perhaps believe we can't do it without new tools. I don't yet, I know we can if we fight hard enough—but it is so much easier to get up steam over a new thing!" Tarbell's letter to Baker, written in February of 1912, also showed an excellent insight into the crucial shift in antitrust philosophy and the probable fate of the antitrust movement:

Do you realize that the shifting of the question [trusts] to one of new governmental machinery [an independent regulatory commission] is going to do for the trust . . . question what the Panic of '93 & the Spanish American war did—Turn attention from them? While we are fighting over the kind of vote with which to dislodge the enemy, the enemy will do as it did in 93–4–5 & again in 97–8—He built his entrenchment higher.[44]

Tarbell's warning carried even greater impact if consideration was given to the fact that the desire of the trusts for such a federal law appeared all but unanimous.[45]

Tarbell also pointed out the abuses of corporate power to consumers and warned corporate directors that consumers were not powerless. During the Pujo Committee's investigation of the "Money Trust" in 1913, she wrote an article in which she accused J. P. Morgan in particular, and all directors of giant corporations in general, of committing the modernizing sin of removing himself from the implications of his actions. She said of Morgan:

It is in his apparent ignorance of the relation between the great enterprises he conducts . . . and the man who buys his coal by the basketful, [or] who must pinch for a year to buy a harvesting machine, that the foundation of the popular mistrust of his power lies. Mr. Morgan . . . has . . . little or no sense of a personage with whom the rich and powerful must at last deal fairly or fall, and that is the "ultimate consumer."[46]

The consumer had the potential to discipline the actions of corporations if methods of trust control remained democratic in nature.

Newspapers that supported a vigorous antitrust policy echoed the sentiments of Tarbell and rejected the idea of government regulation as an alternative to the aggressive enforcement of antitrust statutes. Corporate requests for governmental supervision were, to the *St. Louis Post-Dispatch*, merely pleas for immunity from antitrust prosecutions. Regulation was synonymous with the legalization of monopoly and, by result, the guarantee by the government of trust profits. Such a development would place government in a partnership with business. The consequences were self-evident. "With the power to . . . crush or encourage competition, to fix prices and determine profits, how long would it be before the administration and the trusts would enter into mutually beneficial compacts?" The political consequences to citizens were also apparent. "The corporations might intimidate the party in power by threatening to join forces with the opposition. Before every election there would be a competition between political parties for the favor of great interstate corporations with their vast influence and organization. Government would become the mere instrument of business greed." Consumers would also be at the mercy of this combination of politicians and monopolists. "Competition would be crushed and the opportunity to compete destroyed. The prices of the necessaries of life could be raised or lowered at the will of the men in power." "Every citizen, every household could feel the pinch of ruthless power wielded by greedy monopolists whose eagerness to exploit the public has been proven." In the opinion of newspapers like the *Post-Dispatch*, the economies and efficiency that came from corporate consolidation were "dear-bought" if the power to control production, prices, wages, competition, and the political process itself was placed in the hands of a few.[47]

The questions raised by the *Post-Dispatch* really underscored the underlying grievances of consumers, taxpayers, small retailers, and workers who chose to resist the forces of monopoly. Whether they viewed the rapid economic changes taking place in society from a "modern" or from a more "traditional" perspective, they all sought to preserve older ways of living, working, and of doing business. The loss of what to them were basic social, economic, and political freedoms led them to regard the growth of industrial capitalism as an anti-democratic process. Corporations possessed the economic power to control production and consumption as well as the power to manipulate the political system. To anti-monopolists, such power had been used to distort the true meaning of democracy.

EPILOGUE

In 1915 Benjamin Parke DeWitt attempted a contemporary definition of the "Progressive Movement" in which he sought "to give form and definiteness to a movement which is, in the minds of many, confused and chaotic." To DeWitt, progressivism seemed to be bounded by three cohesive tendencies: (1) opposition to special interests (especially against the influences of large corporations on the political process); (2) more direct, democratic participation by voters in the political process; and (3) a greater degree of governmental action in seeking to bring about economic and social justice in society.[1] Today historians still appear somewhat "confused and chaotic" in their attempts to confront the dilemma first posed by DeWitt. This has prompted historian Daniel T. Rogers once again to go "In Search of Progressivism." After a thorough study of the literature, Rogers, too, arrived at three distinct tendencies: (1) anti-monopolism; (2) "the social bonds and the social nature of human beings"; and (3) social efficiency that offered a distinctiveness to a unique period of American reform.[2] The one thing both agree on though is the need for public control over the new form of corporate consolidation, the trust. The suggestive definitions of DeWitt and Rogers can, I think, help both in assessing the present study, and in allowing it to be placed in the context of Progressive Era historiography.

Anti-monopolism was, as this study has shown, a major concern of many Americans during the late 19th and early 20th century. Building upon an anti-monopoly tradition in America

that dated back to the 17th century, popular resistance to monopoly greatly increased in an industrializing post-Civil War
society. The agrarian-led anti-monopoly movement broadened
its base during the 1890s as the surge of new urban-industrial
monopolies added a new dimension to the growth of industrial
capitalism. Soon a new element, the urban consumer, joined
the anti-monopoly movement. The growth of municipal services directly affected consumers as to the price, quality, safety,
and efficiency of goods and services. The severity of the
depression underscored the vulnerability of urban consumers
and taxpayers to the forces of large-scale industrial capitalism.
Investigative reporting and energetic prosecutions uncovered
examples of corporate arrogance, tax evasion, stolen profits, and
special privilege, and helped to focus the public's understanding of the trust process. After 1897, wide-spread price increases
on the necessities of life compounded those problems. As the
nation formally entered the Progressive Era, trust control over
production, marketing, and consumption reminded workers,
small retailers, and consumers that they had common interests
and a common enemy. The boycott provided a link for producers and consumers in the popular anti-monopoly tradition, and
offered consumers, workers, and small retailers a means of co-
operatively resisting the trust process.

The popular impulse behind the anti-monopoly movement was
a democratic one. People defined democracy in the broadest
possible sense, endowing it with economic and social, as well
as political, implications. They felt that economic injustices were
severe, that their anger was justified, and that popular solutions were both possible and imperative. The popular anti-monopoly movement reflected this attitude. People wanted the
political process kept from the imposing grasp of corporations
and returned to them. They were, in effect, laying claim as the
rightful heirs to the origins and basis of democracy. They hoped
to see the concept of "special privilege" replaced with the more
socially democratic and majoritarian concept of the "public interest." This was central to their definition of freedom and a
prerequisite for any democratic society. Mutuality would re-
place selfishness and give new meaning to mass politics. People hoped to see the economic and political circumstances of

their existence, those which were dominated by the process of industrialization and controlled by immense concentrations of corporate wealth and power, returned to a more equitable and responsible basis. Monopolistic combinations would have to be broken up, restraints of trade removed, price-fixing eliminated, and corporate directors held accountable. If that could be accomplished, then prices could be made more reasonable, wages fair, product quality improved, and services safe. The life, liberty, health, limb, or goods of one man would not, thereby, be impaired by another.

Implicit within the idea of a democratic society was the belief that it could only be maintained and protected if the people regained a sense of community. In an increasingly interdependent society this meant expressing their common grievances, discovering new social bonds, and cooperating. In their fight against monopoly, consumers, workers, and small businessmen adopted the technique of direct, mass participation. This included use of the consumer boycott. They boycotted when trust control over trade, product quality, and prices forced them to curtail purchases of beef or to alter their diets, or when it forced them to modify their methods of doing business. They did this again when Standard Oil controlled the production and marketing of petroleum, and when an urban traction company monopolized an essential municipal service. People also strengthened their social bonds in other ways. They sang songs, wore badges, took part in parades, rioted, petitioned, pledged, and confiscated property as forms of popular protest and community action. They felt a common cause, utilized a mass base of support, and championed the public interest.

Anti-monopolists also urged a greater degree of governmental involvement and intervention in the economy. Governors and state attorneys general called regional antitrust conferences and conventions, and actively investigated alleged corporate wrongdoing. State lawmakers constantly revised antitrust statutes, passed supporting anti-corporate legislation, and even considered state ownership as an option in their fight against monopoly. Finally, President Theodore Roosevelt involved the federal government as he revived the Sherman Act, created the Bureau of Corporations, and provided an aggressive rhetoric of corporate restraint. The public saw hope that the antitrust laws—through trial, fines, and corporate ouster—would be rigidly enforced.

Governmental involvement, however, also brought with it advocates of co-optation. After the Panic of 1907, "trust-busting" lost credibility as a program. As the panic turned into a depression of 1908, critics of Roosevelt's policies gained support from business and financial journals and strengthened their argument that the government needed to alter its antitrust position. Businessmen, frightened by the economic downswing, urged politicians to alter antitrust policy as a step toward restoring business confidence and economic stability. Some leaders of corporate capitalism undoubtedly saw an opportunity to capture dissent as well. Historian James Weinstein has suggested that one of the purposes of the National Civic Federation's Conference on Trusts and Combinations, held in Chicago in October of 1907, was to "divert political agitation against 'monopoly.' "[3] Politicians also sensed a new frustration with an old policy, as well as an urgent need to cooperate with business interests to promote sustained economic recovery.

After 1907, federal and state regulation became the new antitrust panacea and quickly assumed the character of social efficiency. Guided by bureaucratic elites that endeavored to design and control a more rational trust policy, policymakers increasingly viewed corporate consolidation in terms of economic growth and expansion. This triumph of regulation came late to the anti-monopoly movement, and brought with it new pluralistic, interest-group appeals. Administrative solutions, such as the establishment of federal regulatory commissions, offered a means by which those competing interests could be controlled. For proponents of the new regulatory environment to successfully promote their program, they also had to discredit the old one. Businesses reminded consumers that increased costs were always passed on to them and stressed the importance of stability in the marketplace. Corporations warned employees of job security if states ousted their companies. And state officials cautioned taxpayers that lost state revenues meant increased taxes for them. In addition, legal costs were prohibitive, continuous antitrust litigation was disruptive to business in general, and previous policies had not curbed corporate consolidation. But in the larger sense it was a popular movement that was discredited. Aggressive democracy was found to be chaotic, futile, and incompatible with an efficient, modern, growth-oriented society.

One consequence of the shift to regulation and an increased reliance on bureaucratic and administrative solutions to problems has been a feeling of frustration that pervades current-day perceptions of one's ability to bring about meaningful change, or to influence "the system." People today are constantly informed by their culture that only experts and elected representatives are capable of deciding complex issues in the tangled environment of interest-group politics. Such a system encourages deference. Since the shock of the depression of the 1930s, the recurring recessions since then have constantly reminded people of society's very fragile economic superstructure. This has encouraged an inward turn to material concerns and security, reinforced the rationale to trust the economic experts, and strengthened the argument in support of growth-oriented economic programs. Should an aggressive environmental movement, for example, challenge the values of efficiency, growth, and material consumption by suggesting that the net results of such priorities are waste and the destruction of man and the survival of society as a whole, they are confronted with what has become the standard rationale of 20th century social efficiency. Environmental controls or technological restraints mean destitution for manufacturers, lost jobs for workers, rising prices for consumers, governmental subsidies paid for by taxpayers, and a reduced index of growth as a nation. The result has become life under the dark cloud of economic uncertainty and a narrowing of possible options. What has been lost in this process has been a very rich progressive tradition of opposition to special interests; a more direct, democratic participation in the political process; a continued governmental commitment to bring about economic and social justice in society; a vibrant sense of community; and an expansive sense of economic, social, and political possibilities.

NOTES

INTRODUCTION

1. Any of the following studies would fall into this general category. Oswald Knauth, "The Policy of the United States towards Industrial Monopoly," *Studies in History, Economics and Public Law, No. 2* (Whole No. 138), ed. by the Faculty of Political Science of Columbia University (New York: Columbia University Press, 1913), LVI, 175–404; Jeremiah W. Jenks and Walter E. Clark, *The Trust Problem* (Garden City, N.J.: Doubleday, Doran and Co., 1929); Henry R. Seager and Charles A. Gulick, Jr., *Trust and Corporation Problems* (New York: Harper and Bros., 1929); J. D. Clark, *The Federal Trust Policy* (Baltimore: Johns Hopkins Press, 1931); Hans B. Thorelli, *The Federal Antitrust Policy* (Baltimore: Johns Hopkins Press, 1955); William Letwin, *Law and Economic Policy: The Evolution of the Sherman Antitrust Act* (New York: Random House, 1965).

2. Russell B. Nye, *Midwestern Progressive Politics* (New York: Harper and Row, 1965), 4.

3. Engrossing is the buying up of all or a large part of a commodity by one or a number of persons in order to enhance the price by controlling or limiting the supply. Forestalling is the private purchase of goods before they reach the market, or any activity misleading a seller or disuading him from bringing his goods to market.

4. Franklin D. Jones, "Historical Development of the Law of Business Competition," *Yale Law Journal* 36 (November, 1926), 42–55; Vernon A. Mund, *Open Markets* (New York: Harper and Bros., 1948), 111–14.

5. William Trimble, "The Social Philosophy of the Loco-Foco Democracy," *American Journal of Sociology* 26 (May, 1921), 705–15; F.

Byrdsall, *The History of the Loco-Foco or Equal Rights Party* (New York: Burt Franklin, 1967), 101, 110, 112.

6. Chester McArthur Destler, "Western Radicalism, 1865–1901: Concepts And Origins," *Mississippi Valley Historical Review* 31 (December, 1944), 337–38.

7. While acknowledging the increasingly dependent circumstances imposed on the American worker by the growth of industrial capitalism, Herbert Gutman has documented the continued resistance of preindustrial, working-class cultures to this process. See Herbert G. Gutman, *Work, Culture, and Society in Industrializing America* (New York: Alfred A. Knopf, 1976), 3–78.

8. See David Montgomery, *Workers' Control in America* (Cambridge: Cambridge University Press, 1979), 9–31.

9. See David P. Thelen, "Social Tensions and the Origins of Progressivism," *Journal of American History* 56 (September, 1969), 323–41.

10. For a discussion of the alienation of consumption from production, the effort by consumers to restore control over producers, and the importance of this concept for progressivism, see David P. Thelen, "Patterns of Consumer Consciousness in the Progressive Movement: Robert M. La Follette, the Antitrust Persuasion, and Labor Legislation" in Ralph M. Aderman ed., *The Quest for Social Justice* (Madison: University of Wisconsin Press, 1983), 19–47.

CHAPTER 1

1. The technical differences in the definitions of such terms as pools, combines, rings, and later, trusts, were blurred in common usage, and they were used interchangeably to designate the process which "monopoly" broadly encompassed.

2. John D. Hicks, *The Populist Revolt: A History of the Farmers' Alliance and the People's Party* (Minneapolis: University of Minnesota Press, 1931), 63.

3. Solon Justus Buck, *The Granger Movement: A Study of Agricultural Organization and Its Political, Economic and Social Manifestations, 1870–1880* (Lincoln: University of Nebraska Press, 1963), 9–15; Hicks, *Populist Revolt*, 63, 68–69; Chester McArthur Destler, "Western Radicalism, 1865–1901: Concepts and Origins," *Mississippi Valley Historical Review* 31 (December, 1944), 338. See also Fred A. Shannon, *The Farmer's Last Frontier: Agriculture, 1860–1897* (New York: Holt, Rinehart and Winston, 1945), 291–328.

4. Hicks, *Populist Revolt*, 78.

5. Buck, *Granger Movement*, 16–18; Hicks, *Populist Revolt*, 75–79.

6. Hicks cited figures from the federal census of 1890 to show that Kansas, Nebraska, North Dakota, South Dakota, and Minnesota ranked at the top of the list of states in the category of per capita mortgage debt. In Kansas the new per capita mortgage debt in 1885 was more than double the amount incurred in 1880. By 1887 the amount had increased threefold. See Hicks, *Populist Revolt*, 23–24. For at least one account that endeavors to discount much of the late 19th century mortgage burden that agrarian radicals placed at the doorstep of avaricious money-lenders on the Great Plains, see Allan G. Bogue, *Money at Interest: The Farm Mortgage on the Middle Border* (New York: Russell and Russell, 1968). Bogue offers a case study approach to suggest that the Populists disingenuously equated the mortgage with economic misfortune, and failed to concede that it could fulfill a useful and productive function for the debtor.

7. Roger Ransom and Richard Sutch, *One Kind of Freedom: The Economic Consequences of Emancipation* (Cambridge: Cambridge University Press, 1977), 128–31, 149–70, 237–41; Lawrence Goodwyn, *Democratic Promise: The Populist Moment in America* (New York: Oxford University Press, 1976), 26–28; Buck, *Granger Movement*, 18; Hicks, *Populist Revolt*, 21–24, 81–84; Shannon, *Last Frontier*, 291–328.

8. Buck, *Granger Movement*, 53.

9. Ibid., 53, 123–205; Shannon, *Last Frontier*, 329–48. Buck's original claim (1913) that regulation resulted from general agrarian discontent has not gone unchallenged. More recent studies of the problem have emphasized the influence of merchants and shippers on the resulting legislation. See Lee Benson, *Merchants, Farmers and Railroads: Railroad Regulation and New York Politics, 1850–1887* (Cambridge, Mass.: Harvard University Press, 1955), 24–25; George H. Miller, *Railroads and the Granger Laws* (Madison: University of Wisconsin Press, 1971), 161–71, 196; Ari and Olive Hoogenboom, *A History of the ICC: From Panacea to Palliative* (New York: W. W. Norton Co., 1976), 6–10.

10. Homer Clevenger, "Agrarian Politics in Missouri, 1880–1896" (unpublished Ph.D. dissertation, University of Missouri, 1940), 14.

11. Arthur Power Dudden, "Anti-monopolism 1865–1890: The Historical Background and Intellectual Origins of the Anti-trust Movement in the United States" (unpublished Ph.D. dissertation, University of Michigan, 1950), 300, 310–12; Buck, *Granger Movement*, 247, 260, 267–72; Shannon, *Last Frontier*, 329–48.

12. This grass roots beginning was duplicated in other states as well. In Missouri the first Wheel began in Mississippi County in 1886. The state organization was perfected in 1887, and, by August, 1888, the Missouri Wheel claimed 129 locals and almost 6,000 members. St. Louis Journal of Agriculture, ed., *History of the Farmers' Alliance, the Agricul-*

tural Wheel, the Farmers' and Laborers' Union, the Farmers' Mutual Benefit Association, the Patrons of Industry, and other Farmer Organizations (St. Louis: Farmers' and Laborers' Union of Missouri, 1890), 199–200; Clevenger, "Agrarian Politics," 89.

13. W. Scott Morgan, *History of the Wheel and Alliance, and the Impending Revolution* (St. Louis: C. B. Woodward Co., 1891), 55.

14. Dudden, "Anti-monopolism," 321; Hicks, *Populist Revolt*, 111–12; Morgan, *Impending Revolution*, 55–92, 168. The first subordinate Farmers' Alliance in Missouri was organized by agents (deputies) of the National Farmers' Alliance and Cooperative Union. The earliest activity took place in Southwest Missouri, on October 4, 1887, when an organizational meeting was called at Popular Bluff, Missouri. At the time of the second annual meeting in Nevada, Missouri, on August 21, 1888, 615 charters had been issued and membership exceeded 13,000. Journal of Agriculture, *History*, 205; Morgan, *Impending Revolution*, 120–21.

15. Goodwyn, *Democratic Promise*, 43.

16. Ibid., 39; Dudden, "Anti-monopolism," 323.

17. *The Newspaper* (California, Mo.), February 24, 1887.

18. Ibid., January 20, 1887.

19. *St. Louis Post-Dispatch*, December 9, 1887.

20. Clevenger, "Agrarian Politics," 47.

21. Hicks, *Populist Revolt*, 79.

22. Morgan, *Impending Revolution*, 681. See also C. Vann Woodward, *Origins of the New South, 1877–1913* (Baton Rouge: Louisiana State University Press, 1951), 186–87.

23. Luther Conant, Jr., "Industrial Consolidations in the United States," *American Statistical Association* 7 (March, 1901), 2–4.

24. Hicks, *Populist Revolt*, 133; *St. Louis Post-Dispatch*, September 16, 1888; Sanford Daniel Gordon, "Public Opinion as a Factor in the Emergence of a National Anti-Trust Program, 1873–1890" (unpublished Ph.D. dissertation, New York University, 1953), 117, 171, 200, 210; Goodwyn, *Democratic Promise*, 144–45; C. Vann Woodward, *Tom Watson: Agrarian Rebel* (New York: Oxford University Press, 1972), 140–42.

25. Gordon, "Public Opinion," 211–12; Goodwyn, *Democratic Promise*, 105; *St. Louis Post-Dispatch*, March 8, 24, 1889.

26. Gordon, "Public Opinion," 229.

27. *St. Louis Post-Dispatch*, May 18, 1887.

28. Ibid., April 9, May 4, 18, 1887.

29. Ibid., May 21, 1887.

30. Ibid., May 4, 17, 18, 21, 24, 25, 26, 28, June 1, 6, 1887.

31. Ibid., November 29, December 9, 23, 1887.

32. Ibid., December 9, 1887.

33. Ibid., January 13, 1888.

34. Ibid., December 9, 18, 1887.

35. Ibid., May 10, 19, 1888; January 6, March 9, 1889.

36. Ibid., September 10, 1888.

37. On February 24, 1889, a Kansas Senate Committee on the beef combine investigation released their findings. The committee failed to find positive proof of the existence of the alleged combine. They did state, however, that the market was centralized and that a few packers had the power to harm the stock growers of the state. Ibid., February 24, 1889.

38. Ibid., February 7, 1889.

39. Ibid., May 11, 1888; February 7, 8, 10, 17, 1889; *Jefferson City Weekly Tribune*, February 13, 1889.

40. The list of states included Kansas, Missouri, Texas, Colorado, Nebraska, Minnesota, Iowa, Wisconsin, Indiana, and Illinois.

41. *St. Louis Post-Dispatch*, March 12, 1889.

42. Ibid., March 13, 14, 1889.

43. Ibid., March 14, 1889.

44. *The Newspaper*, January 20, 1887.

45. Norman J. Ware, *The Labor Movement in the United States, 1860–1895* (New York: D. Appleton and Co., 1929), 366–67; Gerald N. Grob, *Workers and Utopia: A Study of Ideological Conflict in the American Labor Movement, 1865–1900* (Evanston, Ill.: Northwestern University Press, 1961), 92–98; Hicks, *Populist Revolt*, 136, 139–40; Goodwyn, *Democratic Promise*, 67–69. To complement its growing political influence, the Farmers' Alliance made one other major organizational step when it formally merged with the Agricultural Wheel in December of 1888.

46. Lee Meriwether, "Remarks Made by Lee Meriwether At The Mass Meeting Of Labor Unions And Workingmen At Central Turner Hall, St. Louis, March 5, 1891" (privately published), 4.

47. Lee Meriwether, "A Century of Labor in Missouri," *Missouri Historical Review* 15 (October, 1920), 174.

48. Alexander A. Lesueur, *The Official Manual of the State of Missouri, 1889–1890* (Jefferson City: Tribune Printing Co., 1889), 131. Democrats in Missouri had long been aware of Granger popularity, and had periodically adopted portions of the Granger platform. When the "Young Democrats" revolted against the older conservatives in the party and seized control in the late 1880s, they used the issue of the railroad monopoly and rate regulation to gain farmer support. Then, when the commercial element from among the "Young Democrats," led by David R. Francis, became the conservatives, they clung to control of party machinery only by acquiescing to the farmer-led reforms of 1889 and

1891. Clevenger, "Agrarian Politics," 17, 89, 95, 328; David D. March, *The History of Missouri* (New York: Lewis Historical Publishing Co., 1967), II, 1167.

49. Lesueur, *Official Manual*, 141.

50. In the election of 1890 members of the Farmers' Alliance agreed not to support any candidate who refused to sign a pledge to support Alliance demands. Out of 174 members of the 36th General Assembly, 140 signed the pledge. The Missouri legislature ultimately enacted several anti-corporate measures, including an amended antitrust law. March, *History of Missouri*, 1171–72.

51. Sarah Guitar and Floyd C. Shoemaker, eds., *The Messages and Proclamations of the Governors of the State of Missouri* (Columbia: State Historical Society of Missouri, 1926), VII, 221.

52. James O. Allison, a Democrat from Ralls County, originally wrote the final bill and introduced it in the Missouri House. Allison's measure was a substitute for thirteen other bills on the same subject introduced by as many different members from all parts of the state. *St. Louis Republic*, May 5, 1889.

53. The corporate fine was set at not less than one percent of the capital stock of the corporation or the amount invested in such company, and could not exceed 20 percent of such capital stock or amount invested. Corporate officials could be fined from $500 to $5,000, and might be imprisoned for up to one year. *Laws of Missouri, Thirty-Fifth General Assembly* (Jefferson City, 1889), 96–98.

54. Lesueur, *Official Manual*, 57–59; Homer Clevenger, "The Farmers' Alliance in Missouri," *Missouri Historical Review* 39 (October, 1944), 29; *Journal of the House of the Thirty-Fifth General Assembly of Missouri* (Jefferson City: Tribune Printing Co., 1889), 952–53; *Journal of the Senate of the Thirty-Fifth General Assembly of Missouri* (Jefferson City: Tribune Printing Co., 1889), 925; *St. Louis Post-Dispatch*, April 15, May 4, 1889.

55. The list of states with pre-Sherman Act antitrust laws included: Kansas, Maine, North Carolina, Tennessee, Michigan, Kentucky, South Dakota, Mississippi, North Dakota, Nebraska, Iowa, Missouri, and Texas. The states with antitrust clauses in their state constitutions included: Arkansas, Connecticut, Georgia, Idaho, Maryland, Montana, Washington, and Wyoming. Henry R. Seager and Charles A. Gulick, Jr., *Trust and Corporation Problems* (New York: Harper and Bros., 1929), 341–42. See also *Laws of Missouri, Thirty-Fifth General Assembly*, 96–98.

CHAPTER 2

1. *St. Louis Post-Dispatch*, September 26, 1889.

2. Ibid., November 12, 1889.

3. Ibid., November 9, September 26, 1889; *Jefferson City Tribune*, February 12, 1890.

4. *St. Louis Post-Dispatch*, November 26, 1889.

5. Ibid., February 22, 1890.

6. The state immediately appealed the decision. The case ultimately went to the Missouri Supreme Court where, two years later, it upheld the lower court's ruling. Ibid., November 15, 25, December 8, 1889; January 11, February 22, March 11, 1890; March 14, 1892.

7. In the 36th General Assembly, which convened in January of 1891, farmers comprised 32 percent of the legislators in the Senate and 59 percent in the House. Alexander A. Lesueur, *Official Manual of the State of Missouri, 1891–1892* (Jefferson City: Tribune Printing Co., 1891), 111–15.

8. Figures quoted from the State Auditor's Report showed that railroads operating in Missouri were assessed at less than $60,000,000, while the Report of the Board of Railroad Commissioners indicated that the gross earnings for such roads in 1890 were in excess of $34,000,000 or more than 50 percent of their assessed wealth. *St. Louis Post-Dispatch*, January 14, 1891.

9. A "foreign" corporation was any concern that had its original charter of incorporation under the laws of a state other than Missouri. Ibid., January 8, 13, 14, 29, March 20, 1891.

10. The major weaknesses in the 1889 law included the unconstitutional use of judicial power by the secretary of state, the revocation of corporate charters without due legal process, and the return of the affidavit which could be interpreted as forcing an individual to testify against himself. The amended law eliminated the possibility of criminal indictments entirely and required proper proof of antitrust violations by a "court of competent jurisdiction." The penalties under the revised law involved fines and forfeiture of corporate rights and charters. *Laws of Missouri, Thirty-Fifth General Assembly* (Jefferson City, 1889), 96–98; *Laws of Missouri, Thirty-Sixth General Assembly* (1891), 186–89.

11. *St. Louis Post-Dispatch*, December 31, 1890; March 15, 19, April 4, 1891. See also *Laws of Missouri, Thirty-Sixth General Assembly*, 186–89.

12. As an incentive under the law, prosecuting attorneys received monetary compensation for their services in addition to their salaries. In cases in which no appeal resulted, prosecutors received one-fourth of the penalty collected, which ranged from a minimum of $100 to a

maximum of $500. The corporations themselves were susceptible to a
$100-a-day fine for each day they continued to violate the antitrust law.
In cases of appeal to a higher court, the circuit or prosecuting attorney
and the attorney general each received one-eighth of the penalty re-
covered. Fees, however, were dependent upon conviction, and under
an untried law, the precursor of which had failed the constitutional
test in court, no one seemed willing to invest the time and effort. *Laws
of Missouri, Thirty-Sixth General Assembly*, 186–89; *St. Louis Post-Dispatch*, August 25, November 26, December 29, 1891; April 4, 1892.

13. William J. Fetter, a native of St. Charles, Missouri, entered the
insurance business in St. Louis by providing protection for the steam-
boat trade. When the railroads destroyed the steamship business, Fetter moved to St. Joseph and became manager for the underwriters' association in that city. In 1883 he moved to Kansas City and assumed
control of the underwriters' association there. The various insurance
companies in the Kansas City "territory" employed Fetter, paid his
salary, and gave him sole authority to raise and lower fire and tornado
insurance rates in and around Kansas City. *Kansas City Times*, September 3, 1899; *Jefferson City Tribune*, May 9, 1898.

14. *Twenty-Fifth Annual Report of the Superintendent of the Insurance
Department of the State of Missouri for the Year Ending December 31, 1893*
(Jefferson City, 1894), viii.

15. H. Roger Grant, *Insurance Reform: Consumer Action in the Progressive Era* (Ames: Iowa State University Press, 1979), 76–78; *Twenty-Sixth
Annual Report of the Superintendent of the Insurance Department of the State
of Missouri for the Year Ending December 31, 1894* (1895), viii. The insurance department released figures to show that the percent of premiums taken to cover fire insurance losses in 1893 had been an extremely
high 90.02 percent. But during the next three years of the depression,
as rates continued to go up, the percentage of fire loss declined mea-
surably (1894, 71.14 percent; 1895, 50.28 percent; 1896, 49.51 percent).
For exact figures see the 25th–28th annual reports of the insurance department.

16. *Mexico Intelligencer*, August 3, 1893.

17. Ibid., June 1, July 13, August 17, November 31, 1893; *Kansas City
Times*, October 31, 1893; *Slater Rustler*, October 25, 1894.

18. *Mexico Intelligencer*, August 31, 1893.

19. *St. Louis Post-Dispatch*, May 6, 27, 1894.

20. Ibid., June 17, 1894.

21. Ibid., May 6, 27, June 17, 1894.

22. Ibid., October 15, 1894.

23. Ibid., October 21, 24, 1894.

24. Ibid., October 19, 1894.

25. Ibid., November 24, 1894.

26. Governor William Stone signed the law on April 13, 1895. James A. Waterworth, *My Memories of the St. Louis Board of Fire Underwriters* (St. Louis: Skaer Printing Co., 1926), 135.

27. *St. Louis Post-Dispatch*, April 13, 1895. See also *Laws of Missouri, Thirty-Eighth General Assembly* (1895), 237–40.

28. *Kansas City Times*, July 23, 1897.

29. *St. Louis Post-Dispatch*, February 6, 1895.

30. *Sedalia Weekly Gazette*, September 11, 1894.

31. Senator W. F. Lyons told the *Kansas City Times* that he voted in favor of the exemption in the 1895 legislative session because the insurance lobby did such a good job in presenting their case. The lobby asserted that no central agency other than the boards of underwriters existed to oversee building regulations, water pressure, and main (pipe line) capacity. Large insurers in St. Louis apparently liked this "check" on carelessness. An active board of underwriters provided protection to a business that did not over-insure. Some businesses, anxious to burn out, apparently failed to correct faulty chimneys and defective wires. Major businesses probably met the minimum regulations required by the boards and obtained lower rates than otherwise. *Kansas City Times*, August 1, 1897.

32. Harry Chase Brearley, *The History of the National Board of Fire Underwriters* (New York: F. A. Stokes Co., 1916), 293; *St. Louis Post-Dispatch*, February 3, March 12, 14, 20, 1895; Waterworth, *My Memories*, 134–36; Grant, *Insurance Reform*, 79–80.

33. *St. Louis Post-Dispatch*, March 21, 1893.

34. Ibid., March 17, 21, April 14, May 13, 17, June 8, 1893.

35. The U.S. School Furniture Company of Chicago was found guilty of being a trust and a monopoly on March 30, 1895. The Illinois Supreme Court sustained a similar suit against the Distillers' and Cattle Feeders' Company on June 13, 1895. The Circuit Court of Cook County likewise ruled against the American Tobacco Company on May 15, 1897. Ibid., March 30, June 13, 1895; May 15, 1897.

36. Ibid., May 6, 1894.

37. Ibid., February 13, 21, 1895.

38. Ibid., January 5, 1896.

39. Ibid., May 23, October 22, 26, 1895.

40. Ibid., October 27, 1895.

41. Ibid.

42. Almost six years passed without a conviction under Missouri's amended antitrust law. Ibid., January 16, 1897.

43. Texas achieved apparent success against the Standard Oil Company. Georgia seemed to have compelled the Tobacco Trust, the Snuff

Trust, the Potash Trust, the Coffee Trust, and the Match Trust to abandon contracts that attempted to fix prices and restrain buyers. Ibid., December 12, 1895; February 4, 1897; *Kansas City Times*, February 4, 1897.

44. Henry R. Seager and Charles A. Gulick, Jr., *Trust and Corporation Problems* (New York: Harper and Bros., 1929), 343. See also *Laws of Missouri, Thirty-Ninth General Assembly* (1897), 209–12.

45. *Kansas City Times*, February 4, 1897.

46. Ibid.

47. Ibid., July 23, 1897. The 1895 antitrust law exempted cities of 100,000 inhabitants. The 1897 revision did nothing to remove this condition.

48. Ibid., July 30, 1897.

49. *Eighteenth Annual Report of the Bureau of Labor Statistics* (Jefferson City, Mo., 1896), iii.

50. Ibid., iii–iv; Jack Muraskin, "St. Louis Municipal Reform in the 1890s: A Study in Failure," *Missouri Historical Society Bulletin* 25 (October, 1968), 38–49; *St. Louis Post-Dispatch*, November 22, 1896.

51. *Kansas City Times*, August 7, 1897.

52. Ibid., September 5, 11, 1897. The list of rural newspapers included: *Waverly Times, Dover Democrat, Plattsburg Clintonite, Bethany Democrat, St. Clair County Democrat, Caldwell County Democrat, Glasgow Missourian, Pineville Democrat, Joplin Herald, Chillicothe Constitution, Mexico Intelligencer, Lamar Daily Leader, Stanberry Headlight, Joplin Globe, Monroe County Appeal*, and *Jefferson City Tribune*.

53. *Mexico Intelligencer*, September 8, 1897.

54. *St. Louis Post-Dispatch*, September 9, 1897.

55. Waterworth, *My Memories*, 144.

56. *St. Louis Post-Dispatch*, March 8, December 14, 1898; April 7, 18, 1899; *St. Joseph Daily Gazette*, March 9, 1898; *Kansas City Times*, December 14, 1898; *Jefferson City Tribune*, December 14, 1898; Grant, *Insurance Reform*, 81–82; Sarah Guitar and Floyd C. Shoemaker, eds., *The Messages and Proclamations of the Governors of the State of Missouri* (Columbia: State Historical Society of Missouri, 1926), VIII, 363–65.

57. *St. Louis Post-Dispatch*, September 3, 1897.

58. *Jefferson City Tribune*, May 7, 1898.

59. Fetter also testified that in 1894 or 1895 he and the insurance companies determined that the water pressure in Kansas City was insufficient, and that they raised the rate on every piece of property in Kansas City by 25 percent. By this means the insurance trust forced the city to spend tax dollars to increase water pressure. When this had been accomplished, rates were reduced, but by only 12 1/2 percent. *St. Joseph Daily Gazette*, March 11, 12, 1898; *Jefferson City Tribune*, May 7, 1898.

60. *St. Louis Post-Dispatch*, April 29, 1899; *Kansas City Times*, April 30, 1899.

61. *Jefferson City Tribune*, July 1, 1899.

62. "Ouster proceedings" often served as only the formal legal designation of such suits. Legal officials had no intention of ousting all major insurance companies from the state. They merely used that form of judicial procedure to gain what they really wanted—an end to price fixing and conspiracies in restraint of trade and the payment of a fine. *St. Louis Post-Dispatch*, June 30, 1899; *St. Joseph Daily Gazette*, July 1, 1899; *Jefferson City Tribune*, July 1, 1899; *Kansas City Times*, July 1, 15, 1899; *Thirtieth Annual Report of the Superintendent of the Insurance Department of the State of Missouri for the Year Ending December 31, 1898* (Jefferson City, 1899), ix.

63. A list of cities visited included: New York, Detroit, St. Paul, Quebec, Providence (R.I.), Atlanta, Erie (Pa.), Rochester, Syracuse, Philadelphia, Hartford (Conn.), New Orleans, Cincinnati, and St. Louis. *Kansas City Times*, July 1, 1899.

64. *St. Louis Post-Dispatch*, May 5, 8, June 4, 1899. Coincident with the announcement of the Chicago Civic Federation was that of the Anti-Trust League, which decided to hold a major antitrust demonstration in Burlington Park on August 9. The League also announced that its own antitrust conference would be held in Chicago on February 12, 1900. Ibid., July 16, 1899; February 12, 1900.

65. Ibid., September 21, 1899.

66. Ibid.

67. Franklin H. Head, ed., *Chicago Conference on Trusts* (Chicago: Civic Federation of Chicago, 1900), 263–67.

68. *Lexington Intelligencer*, July 8, 1899. General information on price increases (1897–1899) that would support this farmer's findings can be found in, U.S. Bureau of the Census, *Historical Statistics of the United States, 1789–1945* (Washington, D.C.: Government Printing Office, 1949), 231, 234–35.

CHAPTER 3

1. Harry D. Holmes, "Socio-Economic Patterns of Non-Partisan Political Behavior in the Industrial Metropolis: St. Louis, 1895–1916" (unpublished Ph.D. dissertation, University of Missouri, 1973), 31–52.

2. *St. Louis Post-Dispatch*, January 20, 1898.

3. Ibid., May 18, 19, 1899.

4. Ibid., May 18, 1899.

5. Ibid., June 19, 1899; Sarah Guitar and Floyd C. Shoemaker, eds., *The Messages and Proclamations of the Governors of the State of Missouri* (Columbia: State Historical Society of Missouri, 1926), VIII, 547–52.

6. *St. Louis Post-Dispatch*, June 21, 1899. The point that Stephens and the editors seemed to overlook was the difference between private industrial corporations (such as steel) and quasi-public corporations (such as railroads and utilities). Most reformers would have argued that competition was not an alternative to services which were semi-public corporations or legislative monopolies. The alternative to poor service or exorbitant fares was public ownership or regulation. In *Munn v. Illinois* (1877) the Supreme Court ruled that corporations "affected with a public interest" had greater obligations. The obligations of a quasi-public, legislative-monopoly franchise is what the St. Louis consolidation issue was about.

7. Known before as the Central Traction Company.

8. The United Railways Company, on September 20, 1899, acquired the Lindell, Missouri, Union Depot, National, Jefferson Avenue, and Southern Electric Railway Companies. On September 30, 1899, the United Railways Company leased their properties to the St. Louis Transit Company for a term of years ending April 1, 1939. Under the terms of the lease the St. Louis Transit Company was to operate the properties; make the necessary repairs, improvements and extensions; and pay an annual rental. St. Louis Transit Company Papers, 1st Annual Report, December 31, 1900, State Historical Society of Missouri, Columbia. *St. Louis Post-Dispatch*, July 27, 1899.

9. *St. Louis Post-Dispatch*, July 29, 1899.

10. Ibid., March 11, 1900; Frank Foster, "The Streetcar Strike at St. Louis," *Independent* 52 (July 26, 1900), 1782.

11. *St. Louis Post-Dispatch*, April 30, May 2, 3, 1900.

12. Samuel Lee of Detroit was also actively involved in the Cleveland, Brooklyn, and Buffalo streetcar strikes.

13. *St. Louis Post-Dispatch*, May 5, 6, 7, 8, 1900. William Marion Reedy, editor of the St. Louis *Mirror*, felt the former employees were insistent upon dictating how the managers of the company should run their business (whom should or should not be employed). But Reedy also felt that the Transit Company had "paltered" with the union. In his opinion the company recognized the union in order to prevent a strike in March, when the company was preoccupied with a "bond and stock distribution" matter. Once the bond deal went through, the company went out looking for a chance to cause a strike. *Mirror* 10 (May 10, 1900), 15.

14. *St. Louis Post-Dispatch*, May 10, 1900.

15. Ibid., May 11, 1900.

16. Ibid., May 14, 1900.

17. *St. Louis Star*, May 18, 1900.

18. *St. Louis Post-Dispatch*, May 9, 1900.

19. Ibid., May 10, 1900.

20. Letter from Florence to Frank McCallion, in Philibert Family Papers, May 27, 1900, Missouri Historical Society, St. Louis. *St. Louis Post-Dispatch*, May 9, 1900.

21. *St. Louis Post-Dispatch*, June 1, 1900.

22. Ibid., May 12, 13, 16, 20, 1900; *Mirror* 10 (May 17, 1900), 8; *St. Louis Star*, May 23, 1900.

23. *Mirror* 10 (May 17, 1900), 8.

24. *St. Louis Post-Dispatch*, May 15, 17, 18, 19, 1900.

25. The statement also referred to the Transit Company as a "foreign corporation," most of whose stockholders were from outside Missouri. Ibid., May 17, 1900.

26. *St. Louis Star*, May 20, 1900.

27. *St. Louis Post-Dispatch*, May 17, 20, 1900.

28. Members of labor unions disqualified themselves as possemen due to their refusal to ride on Transit Company cars. *St. Louis Star*, June 5, 1900.

29. *St. Louis Post-Dispatch*, May 30, 31, 1900; Foster, "The Streetcar Strike at St. Louis," 1783.

30. At a mass meeting of strikers and strike sympathizers on May 23, the residents of South St. Louis submitted a resolution to the effect that they sympathized with the men and would help them morally and financially. *St. Louis Post-Dispatch*, May 20, 23, June 1, 1900.

31. Ibid., June 2, 1900.

32. Ibid., June 1, 1900.

33. Ibid., May 24, 1900. Stephens' accusations seem to indicate that there were sharp political differences over how to deal with issues raised during the streetcar strike. The threat of party polarization and mounting constituent pressure support the popular explanation for the party's reversal on the franchise tax question at its June convention.

34. Ibid., April 29, 1900.

35. Reedy's *Mirror* found the Democrats alarmed by the prospect of the loss of the labor vote. *Mirror* 10 (June 7, 1900), 2.

36. *St. Louis Post-Dispatch*, June 4, 6, 8, 1900; *St. Louis Star*, June 6, 1900; *Mirror* 10 (June 14, 1900), 1–4. One such bill, known as the Kelly Bill, was introduced in the city council and narrowly defeated by a 7 to 5 vote. It would have provided for the repeal of all franchises of the St. Louis Transit Company. *St. Louis Post-Dispatch*, June 13, 1900; *St. Louis Star*, June 13, 1900.

37. *St. Louis Post-Dispatch*, June 11, 15, 17, 29, 1900. The editorial opinion of Reedy's *Mirror* was that the boycott finally forced the company to terms. *Mirror* 10 (July 5, 1900), 10. The North and South End sections of the city contained the highest concentrations of lower, lower-

middle, and higher-middle-class groups. See Holmes, "Socio-Economic Patterns," 112–45.

38. *St. Louis Post-Dispatch*, July 3, 9, 1900; *St. Louis Star*, July 12, September 12, 1900; Foster, "The Streetcar Strike at St. Louis," 1784.

39. In his efforts to annul the consolidation, Crow charged that such an arrangement prevented certain companies absorbed by the combine from fulfilling contracts previously made with the state of Missouri and the city of St. Louis. The stock-watering charge involved $23,000,000 of the bonded indebtedness of the St. Louis Transit Company. The *quo warranto* proceedings filed in the Missouri Supreme Court sought to have the charters revoked on the grounds that the companies had capitalized for more than was allowed by state law, and for more than the values of their tangible and intangible properties. Crow, also a member of the Board of Equalization, led the effort for reform, favoring the taxation of corporations for their franchise privileges. This would have involved the assessment of the consolidated street railway corporation at its recapitalized value. *St. Louis Post-Dispatch*, July 13, 17, 1900; *St. Louis Star*, January 25, 1901.

40. The Equal Taxation Committee of the Single Tax League obtained the signatures. *St. Louis Post-Dispatch*, July 17, 1900.

41. Rolla Wells, *Episodes of My Life* (St. Louis, 1933), 193–94. See also James Lee Murphy, "The Consolidation of Street Railways in the City of St. Louis" (unpublished M.A. thesis, St. Louis University, 1964), 92.

42. *St. Louis Post-Dispatch*, January 1, 1901.

43. The law forced the State Board of Equalization to adopt resolutions requiring steam, electric, or cable railroads to furnish it with written answers to questions concerning their property for the purpose of taxation. Ibid., April 29, 1901.

44. Ibid., March 8, 9, 1901.

45. Ibid., April 3, 1901.

CHAPTER 4

1. U.S. Bureau of the Census, *Historical Statistics of the United States, 1789–1945* (Washington, D.C.: Government Printing Office, 1949), 235–36; Paul H. Douglas, *Real Wages in the United States, 1890–1926* (Boston: Houghton Mifflin Co., 1930), 205.

2. *St. Joseph Gazette*, April 28, 1902.

3. Hans B. Thorelli, *The Federal Antitrust Policy* (Baltimore: Johns Hopkins Press, 1955), 294–303; *St. Louis Post-Dispatch*, March 9, 1899.

4. *St. Louis Post-Dispatch*, August 20, 1899.

5. Ibid., July 25, 1899.

6. Ibid., August 23, 1899.

7. Federal Trade Commission, *Report on the Meat-Packing Industry* (Washington, D.C.: Government Printing Office, 1919), Summary and Pt. I, 46–48, 237–56; ibid., (1918), Pt. II, 11–17; Rudolf Alexander Clemen, *The American Livestock and Meat Industry* (New York: Ronald Press Co., 1923), 745–67.

8. Federal Trade Commission, *Report*, Pt. II, 13; ibid., Summary and Pt. I, 46; Clemen, *American Livestock*, 748–50.

9. *St. Louis Post-Dispatch*, June 1, 1900.

10. Ibid., November 14, 1901.

11. Ibid.

12. *St. Joseph Gazette*, April 10, 1902.

13. Cited in *Sedalia Democrat*, April 16, 1902.

14. *St. Joseph Daily News*, April 16, 1902.

15. *St. Louis Butchers and Packers' Gazette*, April 26, 1902.

16. *St. Louis Star*, April 29, 1902.

17. *St. Louis Labor Compendium*, May 4, 1902.

18. *St. Louis Post-Dispatch*, May 3, 1902.

19. *St. Louis Republic*, April 27, 1902.

20. *St. Louis Post-Dispatch*, May 4, 1902.

21. *St. Joseph Gazette*, April 26, 1902.

22. *St. Louis Post-Dispatch*, May 3, 1902.

23. *St. Joseph Gazette*, April 14, 1902. State officials also initiated antitrust investigations. Attorney General M. A. Breeden of Utah began proceedings against the alleged Beef Trust in Salt Lake City by requesting statistics of the State Food and Dairy Commissioner relating to the recent advance in the price of meat. *St. Joseph Daily News*, April 26, 1902. In Denver, Attorney General C. C. Post of Colorado began an attempt before the State Board of Equalization to prove that the Armour car lines were owned by the packing company, and, therefore, part of the Beef Trust. His avowed intention was to "assess the beef trust out of the state." *Kansas City Journal*, April 27, 1902.

24. *St. Louis Chronicle*, April 16, 1902.

25. *Kansas City Journal*, April 19, 1902.

26. *Springfield Leader-Democrat*, April 28, 1902. See also *Kansas City Star*, April 14, 1902.

27. *St. Louis Republic*, April 26, 1902.

28. *Sedalia Democrat*, April 20, 1902; *St. Louis Chronicle*, April 23, 1902; *Kansas City Star*, April 24, 1902.

29. *Kansas City Journal*, April 19, 1902.

30. *Mirror* 12 (April 24, 1902), 2.

31. *Kansas City Star*, April 29, 1902.

32. *St. Louis Post-Dispatch*, April 24, 1902.

33. *Kansas City Journal*, April 23, 1902.

34. *St. Louis Republic*, April 25, 1902; *St. Louis Chronicle*, April 30, 1902; *Kansas City Journal*, April 30, 1902; *Sedalia Democrat*, May 4, 1902.

35. Among those summoned were Charles W. Armour (Armour Packing Co.), J. C. Dold (Jacob Dold Packing Co.), O. W. Waller (Swift and Co.), Gust Bischoff (St. Louis Dressed Beef Co.), and Walter Pfeiffer (St. Louis Butchers' Union). *St. Louis Star*, April 29, 1902.

36. *St. Joseph Gazette*, May 2, 1902.

37. Attorneys Frank Hagerman and Alexander New of Kansas City represented the packers. *St. Louis Star*, May 6, 1902.

38. One butcher stated that the prices in St. Joseph had been raised four or five times since January alone. An arbitrator represented the leading packing companies and it was his duty to supervise the accounts of retail dealers with the wholesale houses he represented. A retailer who failed to pay his bill on time, and whose indebtedness has been made known to the arbitrator, would be placed on a delinquent list and allowed future goods on a cash basis only.

39. *St. Louis Post-Dispatch*, May 6, 1902; *St. Louis Chronicle*, May 6, 1902; *St. Louis Star*, May 6, 1902.

40. The Mound City Packing Company and the North St. Louis Packing Company were two firms that had gone under.

41. *St. Louis Chronicle*, May 7, 1902; *St. Louis Star*, May 7, 1902; *St. Joseph Gazette*, May 7, 1902.

42. No general meat inspection had been made since August, 1900, when three of the four St. Louis meat inspectors were discharged to economize. *Springfield Leader-Democrat*, May 7, 1902; *St. Louis Post-Dispatch*, May 8, 9, 1902; *St. Louis Chronicle*, May 8, 1902; *St. Louis Star*, May 9, 1902; *Chicago Tribune*, May 9, 1902.

43. *St. Joseph Gazette*, May 9, 1902; *St. Louis Star*, May 12, 1902.

44. See *New York Times*, May 7, 10, 1902; *Chicago Tribune*, May 7, 8, 9, 10, 1902; *Washington Post*, May 6, 7, 8, 1902. Events in Missouri seemed to have an accelerating influence on investigations elsewhere. On May 10, District Attorney S. H. Bethea in Chicago asked for an injunction against the combination of beef packers. One week after the Missouri hearings the attorney general of New York began an investigation of the Beef Trust in his state. *St. Louis Star*, May 11, 15, 1902; *Kansas City Journal*, May 16, 1902.

45. *St. Louis Post-Dispatch*, May 7, 9, 1902; *St. Louis Star*, May 10, 1902; *Jefferson City Tribune*, May 8, 1902.

46. *St. Louis Chronicle*, May 7, 1902; *St. Joseph Gazette*, May 8, 13, 17, 19, 1902; *Washington Post*, May 8, 1902. See also Herbert G. Gutman, *Work, Culture, and Society in Industrializing America* (London: Cambridge University Press, 1979), 61–62, for a brief discussion of the New

York City riot as a traditional form of protest and a consumer attempt to "punish" those who controlled prices.

47. *Mirror* 12 (May 15, 1902), 3.

48. *St. Louis Post-Dispatch*, May 21, 1902; *Mirror* 12 (May 15, 1902), 3; *Kansas City Journal*, May 27, 1902; *Omaha Morning World Herald*, May 6, 1902.

49. *St. Louis Labor Compendium*, May 4, 1902.

50. Ibid.; *St. Louis Butchers and Packers' Gazette*, May 10, 1902.

51. *St. Louis Republic*, May 5, 1902.

52. The packers charged that evidence they deemed important was not allowed to be submitted, while much that was submitted would have been inadmissable in a court of law. *St. Louis Butchers and Packers' Gazette*, January 10, 1903. The various companies also raised the question that the agents of the companies, even if they did make agreements to fix prices, were not shown to have been authorized by their "principals" to enter into and make such agreements. Commissioner Kinley disagreed: "The local agents of the dressed beef companies did it [fixed prices] and all knew it and their knowledge is the knowledge of their companies and their acts are the acts of their companies." *St. Louis Post-Dispatch*, January 4, 1903.

53. *St. Louis Post-Dispatch*, June 28, 1902; January 4, March 20, 1903; *New York Times*, April 13, 1903.

CHAPTER 5

1. George C. Sikes, "The Chicago Labor Troubles and Their Settlement," *Outlook* 71 (June 14, 1902), 450.

2. For an analysis of beef prices during this period see: Department of Commerce and Labor, *Report of the Commissioner of Corporations on the Beef Industry* (Washington, D.C.: Government Printing Office, 1905), 167–96; U.S. Bureau of the Census, *Historical Statistics of the United States, Colonial Times to 1970* (Washington, D.C.: Government Printing Office, 1975), Pt. I, 213.

3. For a discussion of the idea of a moral economy see E. P. Thompson, "The Moral Economy of the English Crowd in the Eighteenth Century," *Past and Present* 50 (February, 1971), 76–136.

4. J. C. Kennedy, *Wages and Family Budgets in the Chicago Stockyards District* (Chicago: University of Chicago Press, 1914), 58–80.

5. *St. Louis Star*, May 11, 1902.

6. *New York Times*, May 11, 1902. The companies involved in the petition included Armour, Swift, Hammond, Cudahy, Schwartzchild and Sulzberger, and Morris.

7. Ibid., May 21, 1902.

8. *Chicago Daily Tribune*, May 26, 1902; *Chicago Daily News*, May 26, 1902. In 1899 the American Federation of Labor granted a charter to the International Team Drivers' Union, an organization that only admitted to membership team-owners who operated fewer than five teams. Larger team-owners were formally excluded, but the teamsters who worked for those owners were not attracted to a union that seemed more concerned about prices than about wages. The Chicago teamsters defied their international organization, refused to admit owners, and formed their own national union in 1902 which included only teamsters and helpers (a driver who owned the team he operated could join, but if he owned a team driven by someone else, he could not). Each distinct craft within the teaming industry organized as a "local," and each local had city-wide jurisdiction over all workmen of its craft. J. R. Commons, "Types of American Labor Organization: The Teamsters of Chicago," *Quarterly Journal of Economics* 19 (May, 1905), 400–402. See also Gary M. Fink, ed., *Labor Unions* (Westport, Conn.: Greenwood Press, 1977), 369–70.

9. The driver of a one-horse wagon made 16 cents an hour, while one had to drive a team of six horses to earn 25 cents an hour.

10. Commons, "Types of Labor Organization," 408–09; Sikes, "Chicago Labor Troubles," 449–50; *Chicago Daily News*, May 31, 1902.

11. *Chicago Daily Tribune*, May 27, 28, 29, 1902; *St. Louis Star*, May 27, 28, 1902; *Chicago Journal*, May 28, 1902; *Chicago Daily News*, May 28, 29, 1902; *Chicago Evening Post*, May 29, 1902.

12. *St. Louis Star*, May 28, 29, 31, 1902; *St. Joseph Gazette*, May 31, 1902; *Chicago Daily News*, May 27, 1902; *Chicago Daily Tribune*, May 31, June 1, 1902; *Chicago Journal*, May 27, 1902.

13. *Chicago Daily News*, May 31, 1902.

14. Ibid.; *Chicago Daily Tribune*, May 31, 1902.

15. *Chicago Daily Tribune*, May 27, 28, 30, June 1, 1902; *Chicago Record Herald*, May 28, 1902; *Chicago Daily News*, May 30, 1902.

16. *Chicago Evening Post*, May 29, 1902.

17. *Chicago Record Herald*, May 28, 29, 30, 1902; *Chicago Daily Tribune*, May 30, June 1, 2, 1902; *Chicago Evening Post*, May 29, 1902.

18. *Chicago Record Herald*, May 29, 1902.

19. *Chicago Daily Tribune*, May 30, 1902.

20. *Chicago Daily News*, May 30, 1902.

21. Ibid., May 30, June 2, 1902; *Chicago Daily Tribune*, June 1, 2, 1902. A cartoon depicting a packer and one of his steers appeared on the front page of the *Chicago Daily News* on June 4, 1902. The caption had the beef magnate proclaiming: "And I Can't Even Embalm It" [because of the strike].

22. *Chicago Daily News,* June 4, 1902.

23. Ibid., June 2, 3, 4, 1902; *St. Louis Star,* June 3, 4, 1902; *Chicago Daily Tribune,* June 3, 4, 5, 1902; *Chicago Evening Post,* June 4, 1902.

24. *Chicago Evening Post,* June 4, 1902.

25. *Chicago Record Herald,* June 3, 1902.

26. *Chicago Daily Tribune,* June 5, 1902.

27. Ibid.; *Chicago Record Herald,* June 3, 4, 1902; *Chicago Daily News,* June 2, 3, 4, 1902; *Chicago Evening Post,* June 4, 1902.

28. For suggestions concerning the role of women in earlier crowd activities, see Thompson, "The Moral Economy," 76–136. An example of extreme popular defiance to the injustices of consolidated economic power, and one that underscored the moral sensitivities of consumers, occurred during the severe winter of 1902–1903. Coal shortages gripped many parts of the Midwest. Deaths directly related to the shortages of fuel were reported and stories of destitution and suffering circulated by the thousands. As the crisis deepened, people began to question its underlying causes and suspect that a coal combine or trust was hoarding supplies of coal. In Chicago, a special grand jury conducted an investigation. The Illinois Manufacturing Association submitted evidence that thousands of cars of coal in and around Chicago rested idly on tracks labeled "Hold," and fifty subpoenas were served on coal dealers. In such circumstances, consumers revolted. From Muttoon, Pontiac, and Bushnell, Illinois, came reports that coal had been seized in transit and a fair price offered the owners. In Arcola, Illinois, an engine breakdown stopped an Illinois Central train and the townspeople offered to buy the fuel and pay for the freight as well. When the railroad rejected their offer, they immediately expropriated the coal. The Central agent in Arcola telegraphed headquarters:

"The raid is on; the citizens have taken charge."

The reply came back, "Stop it."

"Confound it we can't," the agent replied. "The whole town is on the cars."

The crowd numbered almost 1,000, and clergymen, bankers, policemen, businessmen, and farmers all took part. The raid was orderly, a grand marshall selected, and a weigher appointed to distribute uniform lots and keep a record for future settlement. The entire town united behind the movement and developed its own sense of justice and sensitivity to human suffering. *St. Louis Post-Dispatch,* January 11, 1903.

29. *Chicago Daily Tribune,* June 4, 1902.

30. Ibid., June 4, 5, 1902; *Chicago Daily News,* June 2, 1902.

31. *Chicago Journal,* June 5, 1902.

32. Ibid.

33. *Chicago Daily News,* June 2, 1902; *Chicago Daily Tribune,* June 3,

1902; *St. Louis Star*, June 3, 4, 1902. See also *Chicago Journal*, June 5, 1902.

34. *Chicago Daily Tribune*, June 5, 1902; *St. Louis Star*, June 5, 1902; Sikes, "Chicago Labor Troubles," 449–50.

35. *Chicago Socialist*, June 14, 1902.

CHAPTER 6

1. See Henry D. Lloyd, *Wealth Against Commonwealth* (Washington, D.C.: National Home Library Foundation, 1936); Henry D. Lloyd, "Story of a Great Monopoly," *Atlantic Monthly* 47 (March, 1881), 317–34; Ida M. Tarbell, *The History of the Standard Oil Company*, 2 Vols. (New York: Macmillan Co., 1925); Chester McArthur Destler, *American Radicalism, 1865–1901* (Chicago: Quadrangle Books, 1966), 105–34.

2. Ralph W. and Muriel E. Hidy, *Pioneering in Big Business, 1882–1911* (New York: Harper and Bros., 1955), 40–49.

3. Lloyd, "Story of a Great Monopoly," 317–34.

4. Destler, *American Radicalism*, 105–34.

5. Hidy, *Pioneering in Big Business*, 201–19, 642–52; *St. Louis Post-Dispatch*, March 13, 1892; November 4, 1906. The Elkins Act of 1903 might also be included in this summary. As an anti-rebate measure, it sought to encourage competition by eliminating special favors gained by corporate shippers such as Standard Oil. See John Quentin Feller, Jr., "Theodore Roosevelt, the Department of Justice, and the Trust Problem: A Study in Presidential Policy" (unpublished Ph.D. dissertation, Catholic University, 1968), Ch. 3. Standard Oil opposed the bill establishing the Bureau of Corporations which it regarded as a "vexatious interference with the industrial interests of the country." See Bruce Bringhurst, "Antitrust and the Oil Monopoly: The Standard Oil Cases, 1890–1911" (unpublished Ph.D. dissertation, Claremont Graduate School, 1976), 182–83.

6. Francis W. Schruben, *Wea Creek to El Dorado: Oil in Kansas, 1860–1920* (Columbia, Mo.: University of Missouri Press, 1972), 1–69; Isaac F. Marcossen, "The Kansas Oil Fight," *World's Work* 10 (May, 1905), 6155–66.

7. Schruben, *Wea Creek*, 37–69; Marcossen, "Kansas Oil Fight," 6155–66; Charles Moreau Harger, "Kansas' Battle for Its Oil Interests," *Review of Reviews* 31 (April, 1905), 471–74.

8. W. Scott Morgan, *History of the Wheel and Alliance, and the Impending Revolution*, cited in Norman Pollack, *The Populist Mind* (Indianapolis: Bobbs-Merrill Co., 1967), 30.

9. One of two competing visions of what the market mechanism offers.

10. For an excellent account of the cooperative endeavors of the Farmers' Alliance in Kansas, see Lawrence Goodwyn, *Democratic Promise: The Populist Moment in America* (New York: Oxford University Press, 1976), 102–7, 145, 159, 182–84, 204. For the influence of trusts upon economic conditions for the farmer, see John D. Hicks, *The Populist Revolt* (Lincoln: University of Nebraska Press, 1961), 78–80.

11. Schruben, *Wea Creek*, 37–69; Marcossen, "Kansas Oil Fight," 6155–66; Harger, "Kansas' Battle," 471–74; *St. Louis Star*, April 18, 1905.

12. Marcossen, "Kansas Oil Fight," 6161.

13. *Emporia Daily Gazette*, February 8, 1905.

14. Harger, "Kansas' Battle," 473.

15. Marcossen, "Kansas Oil Fight," 6155–66; Harger, "Kansas' Battle," 471–74; Ida M. Tarbell, "Kansas and the Standard Oil Company," *McClure's* 25 (October, 1905), 608–22; Schruben, *Wea Creek*, 70–99.

16. "The Battle of a Commonwealth Against the Criminality, Rapacity and Extortion of a Great Corporation," *Arena* 33 (April, 1905), 438.

17. *St. Louis Post-Dispatch*, February 12, 1905; F. S. Barde, "The Oil Fields and Pipe Lines of Kansas," *Outlook* 80 (May 6, 1905), 19–32; Harger, "Kansas' Battle," 471–74; Marcossen, "Kansas Oil Fight," 6155–66; Schruben, *Wea Creek*, 70–99; Tarbell, "Kansas and the Standard," 608–22.

18. *St. Louis Post-Dispatch*, February 12, 1905.

19. Ibid., February 16, 1905; Barde, "The Oil Fields," 19–32; Harger, "Kansas' Battle," 471–74; Marcossen, "Kansas Oil Fight," 6155–66; Schruben, *Wea Creek*, 70–99; Tarbell, "Kansas and the Standard," 616–17; Bringhurst, "Antitrust and the Oil Monopoly," 111–29.

20. This action might have been hastened by the fact that the state initiated two lawsuits in addition to the legislation. The first suit was against the Standard and sought to oust it from the state for having failed to comply with the law, which required a license of foreign corporations doing business in Kansas. The second suit was against the Santa Fe Railroad and sought to break the railroad's system of pooling and of offering rebates to major shippers like the Standard. The second suit was instituted under the Kansas antitrust law, but it was understood that the real target was the Standard. *St. Louis Post-Dispatch*, March 19, 1905.

21. President Roosevelt had ordered the Department of Commerce to investigate the petroleum industry as early as November, 1904, to ascertain if the Standard Oil Company was an illegal combination in restraint of trade. But the investigation had gone nowhere until provoked by the activity in Kansas. Ibid., November 19, 1904.

22. Francis Walker, "The Oil Trust and the Government," *Political Science Quarterly* 23 (March, 1908), 18–46; Marcossen, "Kansas Oil Fight," 6155–66; Schruben, *Wea Creek*, 100–134; *St. Louis Post-Dispatch*, February 16, 1905; *Emporia Daily Gazette*, February 15, 1905.

23. *St. Louis Star*, February 17, 20, 21, 1905; *St. Louis Post-Dispatch*, February 18, 1905; *Emporia Daily Gazette*, February 21, 1905.

24. "The Demand for Federal Aid," *Outlook* 82 (February 10, 1906), 284; *St. Louis Post-Dispatch*, March 14, July 2, 1905; *St. Louis Star*, July 7, 1905; *Emporia Daily Gazette*, March 18, 1905; *Joplin News Herald*, December 28, 1905.

25. *Joplin News Herald*, December 3, 5, 12, 1905.

26. Ibid., December 4, 1905.

27. Waters-Pierce was a "home" company chartered in Missouri, while the Standard Oil Company (Indiana) and the Republic Oil Company (New York) were "foreign" corporations. *St. Louis Star*, March 9, 1905; *St. Louis Post-Dispatch*, February 25, 1905; Frank C. Lockwood, "Governor Hadley of Missouri," *Independent* 66 (April 8, 1909), 744; Herbert S. Hadley, "The Standard Oil Company," *Saturday Evening Post* 180 (February 1, 1908), 3–5, 30.

28. *St. Louis Post-Dispatch*, June 21, 1905.

29. H. J. Haskell, "The People His Clients," *Outlook* 88 (March 28, 1908), 719; *St. Louis Post-Dispatch*, May 30, June 21, 23, 1905; *St. Louis Star*, June 21, 23, 1905.

30. *St. Louis Post-Dispatch*, June 29, July 12, 13, 14, 23, 1905; *St. Louis Star*, June 20, 1905.

31. *St. Louis Post-Dispatch*, October 16, November 23, 1905; *Joplin Daily Globe*, November 25, 1905.

32. *Joplin News Herald*, December 17, 1905.

33. Sherman Morse, "The Taming of Rogers," *American Magazine* 62 (July, 1906), 227–38.

34. Hazel Tutt Long, "Attorney-General Herbert S. Hadley Versus the Standard Oil Trust," *Missouri Historical Review* 35 (January, 1941), 181.

35. *St. Louis Post-Dispatch*, January 11, 1906.

36. Ibid.

37. Ibid., January 15, 1906.

38. Ibid., February 19, 1906.

39. Several suits were ultimately initiated in the State of Ohio. On October 19, 1906, a court at Findlay, Ohio, convicted the Standard Oil Company of conspiracy in restraint of trade under the antitrust law of Ohio. Ibid., October 19, 1906; "The Standard Oil Company Convicted," *Outlook* 84 (October 27, 1906), 437–38; "The Ohio Standard Oil Case," *Outlook* 84 (November 3, 1906), 550–51. See also Bringhurst,

"Antitrust and the Oil Monopoly," 26–65, 162–64, for Ohio's antitrust activities against Standard Oil.

40. In 1900 the State of Texas ousted the Waters-Pierce Oil Company on charges of connections with the Standard Oil Company in violation of the Texas antitrust laws of 1889 and 1895. Shortly thereafter the Waters-Pierce Company reorganized under a charter granted in Missouri and appealed to Texas authorities for a permit to reopen business in Texas. It filed an affidavit with the secretary of state, denied any connection with the Standard, and contended that there had been no division of territory. The Missouri hearings pointed out violations of this recharter agreement. *St. Louis Post-Dispatch*, March 19, June 1, 1900; June 12, 1906. See also Bringhurst, "Antitrust and the Oil Monopoly," 66–101, 147–62, for a thorough account of "trust-busting" in Texas.

41. *St. Louis Post-Dispatch*, January 27, March 30, April 28, July 7, August 16, September 12, 21, 1906; Schruben, *Wea Creek*, 128.

42. Walker, "The Oil Trust and the Government," 18–46; *St. Louis Post-Dispatch*, May 4, September 8, October 28, 29, November 15, 1906.

43. *St. Louis Post-Dispatch*, August 14, 1906.

44. Ibid., September 12, 1906.

45. Ibid.

46. One week before Anthony issued his findings Attorney General Charles T. Cates of Tennessee filed ouster proceedings against the Standard Oil Company of Kentucky under that state's antitrust law. On April 11, 1908, the Tennessee State Supreme Court handed down a unanimous decision against Kentucky Standard and ousted the concern from the state. *St. Louis Post-Dispatch*, January 6, 22, February 25, March 12, 17, May 24, 1907; April 11, 1908; Hadley, "The Standard Oil Company," 3–5, 30; *Laws of Missouri, Forty-Fourth General Assembly* (Jefferson City, 1907), 234–35, 377–82. Hadley's contest against Standard Oil is also covered in Bringhurst, "Antitrust and the Oil Monopoly," 130–46.

47. Walker, "The Oil Trust and the Government," 18–46.

48. Ibid.

49. *St. Louis Post-Dispatch*, June 2, 1907; *St. Louis Globe-Democrat*, June 2, 1907.

50. The law seemed to place the burden of guilt on parties only secondarily connected to the trusts, but its object was to drive trusts, not merchants, from the state. Many merchants chose not to run such a risk and took steps to quit handling trust articles. *St. Louis Post-Dispatch*, July 12, 1907.

51. "A Review of the World," *Current Literature* 43 (September, 1907), 237.

52. Ibid., 238.

53. Ibid.

54. Ibid., 235–40; Walker, "The Oil Trust and the Government," 18–46; *St. Louis Post-Dispatch*, August 3, 1907.

55. The Wall Street slump that occurred in August preceded the severe and sustained financial Panic of 1907, which began to take effect in mid-October and continued into 1908.

56. "The Standard Oil Decision and the Stock Exchange Collapse," *Nation* 85 (August 15, 1907), 151–52.

57. Actual sheet music for "Save Up Your Money, John D. Rockefeller Put The Panic On" has been discovered in Stefan Grossman, ed., *How To Play Blues Guitar* (New York, 1967).

58. *St. Louis Post-Dispatch*, August 13, 1907.

59. Ibid., August 20, 1907. See also Bringhurst, "Antitrust and the Oil Monopoly," 173–206, and Feller, "Theodore Roosevelt, the Department of Justice, and the Trust Problem."

60. The attendance at this preliminary conference included the states of Illinois, Indiana, Texas, Missouri, Ohio, Mississippi, Tennessee, and Kansas. The states of Oklahoma, Iowa, Nebraska, Kentucky, Wisconsin, Colorado, Arkansas, and Minnesota also approved the plan.

61. A list of these states included: Alabama, Ohio, Colorado, Indiana, Kansas, Massachusetts, Minnesota, Mississippi, Nebraska, South Dakota, Texas, Illinois, Wisconsin, and Missouri.

62. Edward Alsworth Ross, *Sin and Society* (Boston: Houghton Mifflin Co., 1907), 123. For a discussion of the "criminaloid" type, see chapter 3.

63. *St. Louis Post-Dispatch*, August 11, 12, September 30, October 1, 1907. In December, 1906, "Night Riders" (tobacco growers) in Kentucky and Tennessee offered an example of the potential for revolution as they rose up against the Tobacco Trust and destroyed trust property with fire and dynamite. The extreme actions in Kentucky and Tennessee had broad implications for all monopolies with large investments in exposed property. The Cotton Trust had gins, mills, and large storage houses. The Lumber Trust had sawmills and millions of board feet of finished lumber. And, perhaps most important, the Standard Oil Company had millions of barrels of oil in storage tanks and a vast pipe line network vulnerable to attack. The threat of such violence had been registered by a reporter who wrote from Titusville, Pennsylvania, on November 4, 1878, and referred to the great railroad strikes of the preceding year. "Had certain men given the word there would have been an outbreak that contemplated the seizure of the railroads and running them, the capture and control of the United Pipe Line's [the Standard's] property, and in all probability the burning of

all the property of the Standard Oil Company in the region." Ibid., December 30, 1906; Lloyd, "Story of a Great Monopoly," 327.

64. Prosecutors in ten states and the Oklahoma Territory filed thirty-three separate suits against the Standard Oil combine between 1890 and 1911. Bringhurst, "Antitrust and the Oil Monopoly," 167.

65. The Missouri Supreme Court ultimately found (December 23, 1908) that the Standard Oil Company, the Waters-Pierce Company, and the Republic Oil Company had conspired to regulate and fix prices, to control and limit trade, to prevent competition in buying and selling, and to deceive the public. The Standard and Republic concerns were ousted from the state, while the Waters-Pierce Company was ordered to dissolve but allowed to reorganize as an independent. The state forced each of the three companies to pay a fine of $50,000. *St. Louis Post-Dispatch*, October 25, 1907.

CHAPTER 7

1. George E. Mowry, *The Era of Theodore Roosevelt and the Birth of Modern America, 1900–1912* (New York: Harper and Row, 1958), 219; Frederick Austin Ogg, *National Progress, 1907–1917* (New York: Harper and Bros., 1918), 15.

2. Robert H. Wiebe, *Businessmen and Reform: A Study of the Progressive Movement* (Cambridge, Mass.: Harvard University Press, 1962), 68–72.

3. William Henry Harbaugh, *The Life and Times of Theodore Roosevelt* (New York: Collier Books, 1961), 323.

4. Robert H. Wiebe, "The House of Morgan and the Executive, 1905–1913," *American Historical Review* 65 (October, 1959), 49–57.

5. Mowry, *Era of Theodore Roosevelt*, 134; Harbaugh, *Life and Times*, 155–56, 233, 295–96, 323.

6. Harbaugh, *Life and Times*, 379.

7. Wiebe, "House of Morgan," 57–60; Gabriel Kolko, *The Triumph of Conservatism* (Chicago: Quadrangle Books, 1967), 164–81. Kolko offers an interesting discussion of both Taft's inconsistencies and the co-operative effort of government and business to secure a more stable trust policy premised on some sort of regulation at the federal level.

8. U.S. House and Senate Joint Committee on Printing, *A Compilation of the Messages and Papers of the Presidents* (New York: Bureau of National Literature, 1911), XVI, 7453.

9. Ibid., 7455. Taft might have been just as alarmed over the radical, consumer-motivated actions of citizens and legal officials. Taft never felt comfortable with the methods of confrontation characteristic of direct democracy.

10. U.S. House and Senate, *Messages and Papers of the Presidents*, 7449–58; Harbaugh, *Life and Times*, 379; Ogg, *National Progress*, 66–67; Charles Johnson, "The Attorney General and the Trusts," *Harper's Weekly* 55 (April 22, 1911), 8. On May 15, 1911, the U.S. Supreme Court ruled in the Standard Oil case. Speaking through Justice White, the court seemed to sanction the good versus bad trust interpretation of governmental policy. Not all restraints of trade or contracts or conspiracies were illegal and in violation of the Sherman Act, only "unreasonable" ones.

11. Speech delivered by Herbert S. Hadley before the 2nd Annual Conference of Attorneys General in Denver, Colorado, August 20–21, 1908, Hadley Papers, Western Historical Manuscripts Collection, University of Missouri Library, Folder 836.

12. Statement given by Herbert S. Hadley to the press during the campaign of 1908, Hadley Papers, Folder 900; Lloyd Edson Worner, "The Public Career of Herbert Spencer Hadley" (unpublished Ph.D. dissertation, University of Missouri, 1946), 126–27.

13. Sarah Guitar and Floyd C. Shoemaker, eds., *The Messages and Proclamations of the Governors of the State of Missour* (Columbia: State Historical Society of Missouri, 1926), X, 29–31.

14. *St. Louis Post-Dispatch*, February 14, 1909.

15. Letter from Herbert S. Hadley to President William Howard Taft, February 26, 1909, Hadley Papers, Letter Book 5.

16. *St. Louis Post-Dispatch*, February 14, 1909; Speech entitled "The Rules of Business and the Laws of Men" delivered by Herbert S. Hadley at chatauquas during the summer of 1909, Hadley Papers, Folder 941.

17. Attorney General Rogers of Arkansas had already completed a successful antitrust suit against the International Harvester Company in June, 1906. In September of that same year Attorney General Coleman of Kansas began proceedings against the International Harvester Company for violations of that state's antitrust law. A limited ouster decision was awarded to the state on February 13, 1910. In both cases the alleged trust was charged with making secret arrangements and agreements with dealers and agents prohibiting the sale of any goods made by competitors. *St. Louis Post-Dispatch*, June 19, September 9, 1906; February 13, 1910.

18. These companies were the McCormick Harvesting Machine Company, the Deering Harvester Company, the Plano Manufacturing Company, the Warder, Bushnell and Glessner Company (Champion), and the Milwaukee Harvester Company. U.S. Department of Commerce and Labor, Bureau of Corporations, *The International Harvester Company* (Washington, D.C.: Government Printing Office, 1913), 2.

19. Ibid., 1–37; *St. Louis Post-Dispatch*, March 12, November 12, 1907;

January 26, 1908; November 14, 1911; Eliot Jones, *The Trust Problem in the United States* (New York: Macmillan Co., 1922), 231–59.

20. *St. Louis Post-Dispatch*, June 17, June 26, 1909.

21. Ibid., June 14, September 7, 1910; November 14, 1911.

22. Ibid., March 25, 1911.

23. The State ex. inf. Elliott W. Major, Attorney General v. International Harvester Company of America, 237 *Missouri Reports* 369 (1911).

24. *St. Louis Post-Dispatch*, February 13, 1910.

25. Ibid.; Guitar and Shoemaker, eds., *Messages and Proclamations*, X, 30; "Hadley on the Harvester Case," a news clipping from the *St. Louis Globe-Democrat*, November 16, 1911, Hadley Papers, Scrapbook 30.

26. Taft remained unyielding on this last point. By successfully completing the Standard Oil and American Tobacco Company cases in 1911, and by moving against U.S. Steel and International Harvester that same year, Taft frightened business. Finally, however, under Woodrow Wilson the Roosevelt program was revived. Business accepted the right of the government to regulate, and government agreed to arrange private settlements. On that basis, American Telephone and Telegraph and the New York, New Haven and Hartford Railroad struck a deal with Attorney General James C. McReynolds to escape prosecution. See Wiebe, "House of Morgan," 57–60.

27. *St. Louis Post-Dispatch*, November 26, 1911.

28. "A Notable Trust Decision," *Independent* 71 (November 30, 1911), 1217.

29. Ibid., 1216–17; *St. Louis Post-Dispatch*, November 29, 1911.

30. The Commercial Club had a membership of more than 900 of the principal industrial and business concerns in Kansas City.

31. *Kansas City Post*, April 9, 1913; *Kansas City Star*, March 23, 1913; "Trust-Busting vs. Regulation," *Outlook* 104 (August 2, 1913), 731–32.

32. *Kansas City Post*, March 21, 1913; *Kansas City Star*, March 23, 1913.

33. Senator Clay, a Democrat, initiated the legislative action from Kansas City and not one of the representatives from Jackson County opposed his measure. In St. Louis, Missouri's other major commercial center, the result was much the same. Only two of the seventeen St. Louis representatives who voted on the bill registered a dissenting vote.

34. *Kansas City Star*, March 21, 1913.

35. A news clipping from the *Denver Times*, March 16, 1913, Hadley Papers, Scrapbook 37.

36. Worner, "The Public Career of Herbert Spencer Hadley," 123.

37. Guitar and Shoemaker, eds., *Messages and Proclamations*, X, 113.

38. "Trust-Busting vs. Regulation," 731–32.

39. The vote was 74 to 35 in the House and 25 to 0 in the Senate.

Journal of the House of the Forty-Seventh General Assembly of Missouri (Jefferson City: Tribune Printing Co., 1913), 1544; *Journal of the Senate of the Forty-Seventh General Assembly of Missouri* (Jefferson City: Tribune Printing Co., 1913), 758–59.

40. *Kansas City Times*, March 21, 1913.

41. Guitar and Shoemaker, eds., *Messages and Proclamations*, XI, 114; *St. Louis Post-Dispatch*, April 9, 1913.

42. *St. Louis Post-Dispatch*, March 21, 1913; *Kansas City Times*, March 21, 1913; Worner, "The Public Career of Herbert Spencer Hadley," 122; "Trust-Busting vs. Regulation," 731–32.

43. *St. Louis Post-Dispatch*, April 5, 1908.

44. Harold S. Wilson, *McClure's Magazine and the Muckrakers* (Princeton, N.J.: Princeton University Press, 1970), 279.

45. *St. Louis Post-Dispatch*, July 10, 1909.

46. Ida M. Tarbell, "The Hunt For a Money Trust," *American Magazine* 75 (May, 1913), 16–17.

47. *St. Louis Post-Dispatch*, November 28, 1911.

EPILOGUE

1. Benjamin Parke DeWitt, *The Progressive Movement* (New York: Macmillan Co., 1915), viii, 4–5.

2. Daniel T. Rogers, "In Search of Progressivism," *Reviews in American History* 10 (December, 1982), 113–32.

3. James Weinstein, *The Corporate Ideal in the Liberal State, 1900–1918* (Boston: Beacon Press, 1968), 74.

BIBLIOGRAPHICAL ESSAY

As an historical study of America's past, I have felt it important to endeavor to discover the actions and attitudes of the people who made up that past. The use of newspapers as source material allowed, as nearly as possible, an expression of the emotions and reactions of those people to surface. The extensive newspaper collections of the State Historical Society of Missouri and the Illinois State Historical Library provided not only a wealth of information on Missouri and Illinois, but on the larger Midwestern region as well.

This study began with the popular origins of the anti-monopoly movement and several secondary works are worthy of mention. Solon J. Buck, *The Granger Movement* (Harvard University Press, 1913); John D. Hicks, *The Populist Revolt* (University of Minnesota Press, 1931); and Fred A. Shannon, *The Farmer's Last Frontier* (Holt, Rinehart and Winston, 1945) are dated, but provide an excellent reservoir of examples of popular protest during very difficult times for the farmer. All three studies find Grangers, Wheelers, Alliancemen, and Populists formulating rational responses to changing economic conditions. A more recent and more detailed study of the Populists is Lawrence Goodwyn, *Democratic Promise* (Oxford University Press, 1976) which is excellent on the cooperative nature of a democratic movement. Several unpublished Ph.D. dissertations are also helpful. Homer Clevenger, "Agrarian Politics in Missouri, 1880–1896" (University of Missouri, 1940); Arthur P. Dudden, "Anti-monopolism 1865–1890: The Historical Background and Intellectual Origins of the Anti-Trust Movement in the United States" (University of Michigan, 1950); and Sanford D. Gordon, "Public Opinion as a Factor in the Emergence of a National Anti-Trust Program, 1873–1890" (New York University, 1953) offer three different approaches to the larger topic.

The 1890s proved to be a testing ground for new antitrust legislation at both the state and national levels. Hans B. Thorelli, *The Federal Antitrust Policy* (Johns Hopkins Press, 1955) is the most thorough account of the history of the Sherman Act to 1903. Missouri's first successful legal test of its antitrust law was against the Insurance Trust. Several studies of the insurance industry proved helpful. Harry C. Brearly, *The History of the National Board of Fire Underwriters* (Frederick A. Stokes, 1916); James A. Waterworth, *My Memories of the St. Louis Board of Fire Underwriters* (Skaer Co., 1926); and the Annual Reports of the Missouri State Insurance Department provide the industry point of view. The Kansas City, St. Joseph, and rural Missouri press supplied the perspective of policyholders. H. Roger Grant, *Insurance Reform* (Iowa State University Press, 1979) offers a good overview of consumer reaction in New York, Wisconsin, Kansas, Texas, and Missouri. Franklin H. Head, ed., *Chicago Conference on Trusts* (Civic Federation of Chicago, 1900) assesses the trust problem at the end of the decade from a variety of viewpoints.

On the topic of urban modernization and franchise monopoly as seen in the St. Louis streetcar strike of 1900, the collections of the Missouri Historical Society at St. Louis are helpful. More useful are two unpublished theses by Harry D. Holmes, "Socio-Economic Patterns of Non-Partisan Political Behavior in the Industrial Metropolis: St. Louis, 1895–1916" (University of Missouri, 1973) and James L. Murphy, "The Consolidation of Street Railways in the City of St. Louis" (St. Louis University, 1964). However, the best sources of information on the topic are St. Louis newspapers. The *Post-Dispatch, Globe-Democrat, Chronicle, Mirror, Republic*, and *Star* offer descriptive accounts of the strike as well as incisive editorial comments.

Newspapers from the meat-packing towns of Chicago, Kansas City, St. Joseph, and St. Louis also offer the best information on popular reaction and state-level investigation of the Beef Trust. Rudolf A. Clemen, *The American Livestock and Meat Industry* (Ronald Press, 1923) has useful information on the organization and development of the industry. Charles E. Russell, *The Greatest Trust in the World* (Ridgway-Thayer Co., 1905) presents a muckraker's point of view. The most detailed information on the topic, however, has been provided by the U.S. Government: U.S. Bureau of Corporations, *Report on the Beef Industry* (Government Printing Office, 1920) and U.S. Federal Trade Commission, *Report on the Meat-Packing Industry* (Government Printing Office, 1918–1919).

Chicago newspapers also supplied the body of information on the teamsters' strike of 1902. The *Tribune, Daily News, Journal, Record-Herald, Evening Post*, and *Socialist* are excellent for understanding community involvement, crowd behavior, and the common ground between producers and consumers. E. P. Thompson, "The Moral Economy of the English Crowd in the Eighteenth Century" *Past and Present* 50 (February, 1971), 76–136, offers valuable insights concerning the idea of a moral economy and the role of women in crowd disturbances. John C. Kennedy, *Wages and Family Budgets in the Chicago Stockyards District* (University of Chicago Press, 1914) has detailed information on the standard of living of many working-class Chicagoans.

A vast amount of material has been written on the Standard Oil Trust. Ralph and Muriel Hidy, *Pioneering in Big Business, 1882–1911* (Harper and Bros., 1955) is one of several studies that deals with the organization, operation and growth of the Standard Oil Corporation in a generally favorable manner. Henry D. Lloyd, *Wealth Against Commonwealth* (National Home Library Foundation, 1936) and Ida M. Tarbell, *The History of the Standard Oil Company* (Macmillan Co., 1925) provide critical assessments. E. A. Ross, *Sin and Society* (Houghton Mifflin, 1907) does not attack Standard Oil in particular, but poses an interesting argument in favor of an updated criminal definition of corporate crimes in general. Francis W. Schruben, *Wea Creek to El Dorado* (University of Missouri Press, 1972) is an excellent account of the Kansas oil producers' fight against Standard Oil. An unpublished Ph.D. dissertation by Bruce R. Bringhurst, "Antitrust and the Oil Monopoly: The Standard Oil Cases, 1890–1911" (Claremont Graduate School, 1976) takes a look at anti-Standard activity in Ohio, Missouri, Texas, and other states. Much of the popular periodical literature also followed the activities surrounding Standard Oil. The *Independent, Outlook, Arena, Saturday Evening Post, Review of Reviews, McClure's, Harper's Weekly, Current Literature, Atlantic Monthly, American, Century, World's Work*, and *Nation* all carried informative articles on trust-busting and Standard Oil.

The efforts of policymakers to adopt a rational, efficient, regulatory antitrust policy has intrigued several historians. Roosevelt's approach to the trust issue is dealt with in an unpublished Ph.D. dissertation by John Q. Feller, "Theodore Roosevelt, the Department of Justice, and the Trust Problem: A Study in Presidential Policy" (Catholic University, 1968). Gabriel Kolko, *The Triumph of Conservatism* (Quadrangle, 1967) is helpful on Taft's trust ideas and on attempts by business and government to stabilize trust policy. Business-government cooperation occasionally took the form of gentleman's agreements, and is discussed in Robert H. Wiebe, "The House of Morgan and the Executive, 1905–1913" *American Historical Review* 65 (October, 1959), 49–60. The impact of the Panic of 1907 on the economic thinking of businessmen is touched on in Robert H. Wiebe, *Businessmen and Reform* (Harvard University Press, 1962). The Herbert S. Hadley Papers in the Western Historical Manuscripts Collection of the University of Missouri Library at Columbia are extremely helpful for understanding the shift toward bureaucratization and regulation at the state level. Additional information on Hadley can be found in an unpublished Ph.D. dissertation by Lloyd E. Worner, "The Public Career of Herbert Spencer Hadley" (University of Missouri, 1946).

INDEX

Rockefeller, John D., 106; attacks antitrust policy, 127
Rogers, Daniel T., 152
Rogers, Henry H., 121
Rogers, Robert Lee, 122
Roosevelt's Panic, 132
Roosevelt, Theodore, 131, 143; defends antitrust policy, 127; develops policy of governmental regulation, 132-33; orders investigation of petroleum industry, 115; publicly denounces Standard Oil, 123
Ross, E. A., and criminaloid type, 128-29

St. Joseph Daily News, on price increases, 77
St. Joseph Gazette, on cost of living, 76
St. Joseph News Press, 121
St. Joseph Social Club, 48-50, 136
St. Louis Board of Fire Underwriters, 41
St. Louis Bridge Combine, 43
St. Louis Chronicle, on food trust, 80
St. Louis Civic Federation, 46
St. Louis Gas, Fuel, and Power Company, 24-25
St. Louis Gaslight Company, 24-25
St. Louis Gas Trust, 24-25
St. Louis Ice Pool, 22-23
St. Louis Labor Compendium, 77
St. Louis Post-Dispatch: against railway consolidation, 57-58; on antitrust enforcement, 34, 39-40, 44; on beef combine, 26; on bridge combine, 43; on franchise taxation, 67; on gas trust, 24-25; on ice combine, 23; inter-

view with M. J. Maloney, 42; on municipal tax assessments, 56; opposes idea of governmental regulation of trusts, 150; on price increases, 73
St. Louis Republic, 18
St. Louis Socialist Labor Party, 46
St. Louis Transit Company, 58, 168 n.8
Sayers, Joseph D., calls antitrust convention, 51
Sedalia Weekly Gazette, 41
Sherman Antitrust Act, 4, 123, 157 n.1
Simmons Hardware Company, 34-35
Single Tax League, 46, 56
Smith, Herbert Knox: "Report on the Position of the Standard Oil Company in the Petroleum Industry," 125
Southern: cotton farmers fight jute bagging trust, 19-20; farm debt, 14
South Improvement Company, 106
Springfield Leader and Democrat: on beef prices, 80
Standard Oil Company: appeals Missouri ouster decision, 138, 144-48; early trust agreement, 106; federal actions against, 123, 125-26, 176 n.5, 182 n.10; operations in Kansas, 109-11, 114, 177 n.20; state actions against, 108, 114-15, 122, 125, 178 n.39, 179 nn.40, 46, 181 nn.64, 65
Stephens, Lon V., 48; attacks political opposition, 66; attempts to mediate transit strike, 60; supports railway consolidation bill, 57-58

About the Author

STEVEN L. PIOTT is Assistant Professor of History at the University of Wisconsin Center at Marshfield. He co-authored, with Richard J. Jensen and Christopher C. Gibbs, *Grass Roots Politics: Parties, Issues, and Voters, 1854–1983* (Greenwood Press, 1983) and has contributed articles to *Labor History*, *American Studies*, and *Missouri Historical Review*.